The Arab Mind Bound

TAREK HEGGY

VALLENTINE MITCHELL
LONDON • CHICAGO

First published in paper in 2022 by Vallentine Mitchell

Catalyst House
720 Centennial Court, Centennial Park
Elstree WD6 3SY, UK

814 N. Franklin Street
Chicago, Illinois
60610, USA

www.vmbooks.com

first published in cloth in 2011

British Library Cataloguing in Publication Data
an entry can be found on request

ISBN 978 0 85303 894 8 (cloth)
ISBN 978 1 80371 012 9 (paper)
ISBN 978 0 85303 849 8 (ebook)

Library of Congress Cataloging-in-Publication Data
an entry can be found on request

THE ARAB MIND BOUND

Contents

Preface

In the 1970s I wrote three critical studies of socialism, followed by six more books published in the 1980s on the political, economic and social problems of Egypt and Arab countries adapting the Egyptian model. And then I was afflicted with an acute case of writer's block. For three long years, from 1994 to 1996, for the first time in my life I stopped writing altogether. However, this dry spell was not without its advantages. Indeed, it turned out to be probably the most beneficial stage of my intellectual life. Although I was extremely frustrated at my inability to write at the time, this hiatus allowed me to see the problems plaguing Egypt and other Arabic-speaking countries with more clarity.

Consequently, I discovered that while between 1977 and 1994 I had written dozens of articles and nine books, I had only been writing about the symptoms rather than about the disease blocking progress and inspiring so much violence. Since 1997, all my writings have been focused on the disease. All the political, economic, social, educational and information-related problems in Arab societies are symptomatic of a debilitating disease afflicting contemporary Arab culture, which is unique among world cultures in that it has distanced itself from the march of human progress.

No one can accuse Japan, India, China, Russia and western European countries of being under the tutelage of the world's only superpower at the present time, the United States. But still, they play the game according to the rules dictated by the global balance of power and the strategic realities of the post-Second World War period, which I believe ended with the collapse of the Socialist bloc under the leadership of the former Soviet Union in 1991, rather than with the end of the war in 1945. However, unlike Russia, China, Japan, India and western Europe, the Arab countries, despite their economic and educational weakness and complete dependence on others in matters of security, refuse to play by the rules of the game or in accord with its internal dynamics and mechanisms.

Thus, I have concluded that Arabic-speaking societies have come to form a bloc standing outside the march of human progress because of their current cultural conditions, and not because of any other factor, though I do not deny the existence of a diversity of other factors. The prevailing culture in Arabic-speaking societies today is one of complaining and finger-pointing, blaming others for any misfortune, seeing enemies and conspiracies where none exist or blowing minor existing dangers out of proportion. It is also a destructive, close-minded culture, virtually devoid of any critical thinking, one that does not accept criticism. Other negative features include a tendency to indulge in excessive self-praise, glorification of past achievement and an exaggerated sense of self-importance, not to mention an alarming and unprecedented increase in aggression.

During the last twelve years, I have written many articles and several books in Arabic and English, which, after much rethinking and rewriting, I have now distilled into this book. I consider that Arab culture today is shackled with two heavy chains. At the end of the first chain hangs a heavy iron ball bearing the inscription 'the negative, medieval and regressive understanding of Islam'. On the end of the second chain hangs an equally heavy weight bearing the inscription 'defective thought processes, intellectual distortions and negative delusions that produced the educational systems in Arab societies, rendering them the worst in the world'.

Arab educational systems are based on learning by rote rather than on fostering creativity, research, critical thinking and team work. They are also designed to discourage critical thinking, tolerance, and acceptance of the other, respect of pluralism and diversity, and a belief in the universality of science and knowledge. As a result, they have built high walls between most of the Arab youth and the dynamics of the age in which we live, with its scientific achievements and breakthroughs. They have not provided young people with the skills required to engage in the global game according to the rules currently in force. This turns people into something like football players who withdraw from a match and sit on the sidelines shouting insults at the referee and the players still on the field while absolving themselves of all blame.

Contemporary Arab societies are living a painful reality fraught with danger, not only for themselves but also for humanity as a whole. The only way out of this untenable situation is through an approach that is both political and educational. In politics there is an urgent need for new leadership and constructive initiatives. What is required in education is nothing short of a revolution, involving a complete overhaul of the system, its philosophy, programmes, the nature of teachers and students, and finally the infrastructure generally. An improvement in the quality of leadership can bring about relative gains in both the short term and the medium term; but only an educational revolution can bring about the desired change in the long term.

This book is an attempt to cast light on these two heavy chains shackling contemporary Arab culture: religion and education.

Tarek Heggy
Cairo, 2011

The Lotus Revolution

I finished writing my study of the Arab mind (in two books: *The Arab Cocoon* and *The Arab Mind Bound*) a few months before the outbreak of the revolution of the youth, known as the Lotus Revolution. But in fact, there is a strong link between these two books and the youth revolution in more than one Arab society (Tunisia in December 2010, and Egypt in January 2011). This revolution has proven (especially in Egypt) that there is a new generation, freer and more liberated from the ties binding the minds of the sons and daughters of the Arabic-speaking societies. The Tunisians have lived for close to a quarter of a century under two frightening circles: the circle of the tyranny of the absolute ruler, and the circle of his corruption and that of his junta. But the Tunisians only revolted when a younger generation that learned about the world through modern technology (Internet, e-mail, Facebook, Twitter) matured. This new source of knowledge and culture has enabled the sons and daughters of Tunisia to know that the tyranny and corruption of their rulers was something unnatural which does not exist in more advanced societies.

And in Egypt, the revolution (after three decades of the tyranny and corruption of Hosni Mubarak's regime) did not come from the Islamists, nor did it come from the opposition parties (created by the dictatorial regime), and nor did it come from the poor, the unprivileged or the inhabitants of the slums. The revolution of the youth in Egypt on 25 January 2011 was ignited by the educated sons and daughters of the middle class, who are equipped with the tools of modern telecommunications technology.

I have no doubt that the youth revolution in Tunisia and Egypt will be followed by other revolutions in the remainder of the Arab societies; revolutions that will oust regimes which have reached the climax of tyranny and corruption at the same time. And I have no doubt that these revolutions will simultaneously represent the following: first, the end of the roles of generations outdated by technology (headed by informatics, telecommunications and media technology); these generations have become components of the past. Second, new generations will lead the Arab societies towards progress and modernity, not through ideologies, but through the contemporary tools of technology in diverse fields. Third, the Arab mind, which I have described in my books *The Arab Cocoon* and *The Arab Mind Bound*, will be cured of its evils during the coming decades, at the hands of those who surprised the world by initiating the revolution – and these are the children of the middle class with a modern education, supplied with modern tools of knowledge – and not at the hands of a particular ideology or a (Muslim) Martin Luther who would renew the Muslim mind. I am certain that the revolutions of the youth of the middle class in the Arab societies are what will bring about the required change within the structure of the Muslim mind, Muslim culture and Islamic religious teaching.

Tarek Heggy
February 2011

Part I

The Emergence of an Intolerant Islam

Introduction

There is a version of Islam that was in the ascendant for centuries and is quite different from the image of that religion perceived by many in Europe and America today. It might best be called 'Turkish-Egyptian Islam'. Until the 1940s, this paradigm stood as a unique example of tolerance and flexibility. Outside the Arabian Peninsula, Muslims have always known extremely tolerant societies, in countries like Egypt, Syria, Spain before the sixteenth century, and in North Africa. This doctrine especially prevailed in the Ottoman Empire, a multinational Islamic state founded by tribes of Turkish origin in Anatolia at the end of the thirteenth century.

At its peak, this state, with its capital in Istanbul, comprised most of south-western Asia, the Balkans, Egypt and large portions of the North African coast. It ceased to exist in 1919. Egypt was ruled by the Empire, or at least heavily influenced by its culture, from 1517 to 1882. In this state, non-Muslims enjoyed more protection than any other minority living anywhere else in the world at the time. Christians and Jews shared conditions very similar to the ones in which the Muslim subjects of the Empire were living. Even when certain rulers were repressive, this was a general policy, one of equally bad treatment which made no distinction between non-Muslims and Muslims. As the British-born historian Bernard Lewis has said, the Jews played their greatest roles in history twice: once with the Muslims (in the past), and once with the Christians (in the present).[1]

'Turkish-Egyptian Islam' was noted for its acceptance of the 'Other'. It was not pathologically obsessed with the fine print of scripture. While recognizing the divine character of the revealed laws and the prophetic additions, it also recognized that some of their provisions were formulated to suit the context of a different time, place and varying circumstances. Thus divinity was reserved for religion and did not extend to how mortals understood or chose to interpret its strictures. It was tacitly understood that there is a subjective dimension to the interpretation of any text, and that interpretation is necessarily coloured by the interpreter's predilection shaped by his cultural formation, knowledge and intellectual abilities.

A comparison between Islamic and Arab societies today and those of a century ago reveals how much more widespread a mentality of violence has become in contemporary societies. An even bigger danger is the spread of a culture conducive to its growth and development, spawning militants who nurture this mentality of violence and creating a general climate that allows it to take a firm grip.

There have always been people like this, radical Sunni Islamists such as Sayyid Qutb, Osama bin Laden, Ayman al-Zawahiri and Abu Mus'ab al-Zarqawi, in the history of Islam. Until, recently, though, they were a renegade and marginal minority. The tragedy today is that they are no longer marginal. Their message is reaching huge numbers of people and they are gaining new supporters and sympathizers every day. Why?

Islam can be said to be one of the most important shapers of the culture, way of life, thought processes, opinions and reactions of Muslims. Yet analysts concerned with both diagnosing and curing the problem must define more specifically what this means.

What is the cause and issue here:

- Is it the nature of Islamic Scripture?
- Is it how people interpret scripture?
- Is it Islamic jurisprudence? If so, which school of jurisprudence? Is it Islamic jurisprudence according to Abu Hanifa (699–767); Ibn-Malik; Al-Shafi'i; or Ibn-Hanbal (780–855)[2] and his disciples, notably Ibn Taymiyya (1263–1328),[3] Ibn Qaiyim al-Jawziyya (1292–1350) and the proselytizer Muhammad Ibn Abd al-Wahhab (1703–1792)?[4] Or is it Islamic jurisprudence according to the Shia Imamiyya school, whose most prominent exponent was Ja'far al-Sadiq, (702–765) or to the Khawarij (the Seceders),[5] who were neither Sunni nor Shia and who themselves had four subdivisions?
- Is it historical experience? If so, what particular experience?
- Is it Islam as understood by the Umayyads,[6] who ruled from 660 to 750, or by the Abbasids, who ruled from 750 to 1258?
- Indeed, which Islam?

Can one really talk of a single homogeneous Islamic experience? After all, the experience of Umayyad Damascus was very different from that of Abbasid Baghdad, while both were very different from the historical experience of Andalusia, where a unique bonding between Muslims and Jews produced such great thinkers as the Muslim Ibn Rushd (Averroes, 1126–1198) and the Jewish physician and philosopher Ibn Maymun (Maimonides, 1135–1204).

In truth, scripture in and of itself, means little when invoked out of context. Here the quality, mind and vision of the person dealing with the text are all important.

Since it has existed in so many variations of interpretation and experience 'Islam' cannot be held responsible for the phenomenon of violence, which is a world view created by five factors:

- Political oppression at the hands of autocratic forms of governments marked by a lack of democracy.
- Widespread corruption, the inevitable result of political oppression.
- The rise of the Wahhabi brand of Islam along with the retreat of the tolerant Turco-Egyptian model which had prevailed for centuries.
- The renewed introduction of tribal values which came with the spread of the Wahhabi interpretation of Islam. Islam had tried to abolish tribal loyalties and redirect the loyalty to the Muslim 'super-tribe', namely the whole Umma.
- Educational systems completely divorced from modernity.

NOTES

1. From a personal conversation between Professor Lewis and the author (Princeton, June 2004).
2. Founder of the 'textualist' school.
3. He wanted to take Islam back to its sources.
4. Founder of Wahhabism.
5. They originally supported Ali the fourth Caliph, and then rejected him for his accepting arbitration with his Seffein battle enemies.
6. First Muslim ruling dynasty.

1

The Emergence

I. THE FUEL OF INTOLERANT ISLAM

Many have attributed the spread of religious extremism today in countries like Egypt to external factors, such as foreign incitement and foreign financing of extremist movements in general, and of fundamentalist Islamic groups in particular. This attribution is extremely dangerous, because by presenting the issue of religious extremism as a security problem, to be dealt with by the police and other security bodies, it is removed from the realm of issues amenable to political solutions. Those who are quick to point an accusing finger at external forces should realize that if Egypt had been a haven of social tolerance, brotherhood and peace, it would not have been susceptible to interference from abroad. This means that other, local, factors have created a favourable climate for such attempts to succeed.

A. Political Oppression

Over the last few decades, many societies in Islamic countries were subjected to various types of despotic rulers, governing their countries with an iron fist in the context of widespread autocracy. This led in many cases to a downward spiral. The most dangerous of the many negative effects of political oppression is the impeding of social mobility, frustrating the opportunity for the most qualified citizens to rise to leading positions in various fields.

The disappearance of a healthy process of social mobility makes for a static situation in which inept and mediocre persons come to occupy positions of power and influence by dint of accepting, indeed, of supporting, oppression through unquestioning loyalty to their superiors. In other words, Arab and Islamic societies in general are caught today in an equation which can be called the equation of destruction: oppression and autocracy produce followers, not competent people.

Lack of social mobility destroys competence across the board at all levels of society. Lack of competence in turn results in the collapse of all institutions and in widespread mediocrity which becomes the norm. This engenders a powerful evil energy, namely despair and rage, which breeds the mentality of violence, leading to the devaluation of the worth of human life, whether of one's self or of others, as well as spreading a desire for revenge. This acquired 'mentality of violence' came to permeate many of these societies.

By the same token, oppressors prevent the growth of civil society, generalize incompetence and divide political life into two levels:

- An above-ground level which belongs exclusively to the rulers and their cohorts;
- An underground level which belongs to Wahhabi or other radical versions of Islam, like that developed by the Muslim Brotherhood theorist, Sayyid Qutb,[1] in the 1950s and 1960s.

In the absence of civil society, with the lack of social mobility and the prevalence of incompetence, the stage is set for a new group of oppressors who are at the same time themselves incompetent.

No sooner are there changes causing the downfall and removal of the despotic ruler in these societies (Suharto in Indonesia, Saddam Hussein[2] in Iraq) than there emerge on the scene cadres which fanatically interpret Islam and who come from the only other existing political force – the underground – and who now put themselves forward as saviours! However, they will only lead their societies into greater depths of backwardness, distance them still further from the modern age, and sink them even deeper into social problems.

A valid question here is why this is the only model that emerges whenever an oppressive regime falls in a Muslim or Arab country. The answer is simply that this is a natural result of the widespread despair felt by those living under an autocratic regime that allows no open political activities. Hence, the only organizations that can survive in its shadow are those operating underground. The cure must start with the first link in the chain, not with the last. The educational and media institutions are incapable of redressing this disaster, because they too have been corrupted at the hands of incompetent leadership.

B. Wahhabism and Tribal Values

There are many ways of interpreting Islam. There are four Sunni schools of jurisprudence, then there is the Shia, four main doctrines of the Khawarij, and such interpretive schools as that of the tenth-century Persian historian al-Tabari[3] and the early Egyptian Layth Ibn Saad.[4] Moreover, there were the dialectical theologians the Mutaqalimun, originating in the ninth century, and the contemporary philosophical teachings of the Mu'tazaliyya, who depended on reason, and the tenth century Ash'ariyya, and various secret movements, the Batiniyya.

The point here is not to explore all of these various schools and thinkers but to point out that any effort to reduce Islam to one interpretation and to cast all others as heresy denies the fact that there has been a multitude of perspectives; Islamic texts are amenable to many interpretations. Some of the earliest converts to Islam admitted as much some 1,400 years ago when it was said by Caliph Ali Ibn Abu-Talib, 'The Quran displays many faces'.[5] Again, what counts is the person who reads, understands and presents a textual interpretation. The practice of relying on one text while ignoring another is a destructive process that lends itself to abuse. If one studies Jewish texts like the Torah and the Talmud, it is clear that one cannot take at face value the words spoken by Joshua, son of Nun, on a certain occasion in a given context. By the same token, the dowry cannot be said to be an article of Jewish faith just because King Saul demanded it from David, son of Jesse of Bethlehem (King David for the Jews, the Prophet David for the Muslims) for the hand of his daughter Michal. It is not sufficient to go around brandishing a text as a divine revelation outside its historical, human and chronological framework.

This applies to Islam, too. For example, the sources of jurisprudence and the number of the Prophet's hadiths regarded as sources of religious doctrine and practice vary widely from one school to another. The great jurist Abu Hanifa accepted just over a hundred as apostolic precepts, while the conservative theologian Ahmed Ibn Hanbal accepted over ten thousand in his book *al-Musnad*.

Thus, the followers of the Hanafi school rely on *istihsan* (literally preference, which means using few traditions and extracting from the Quran the rulings which fit their ideas); while the followers of the Maliki school rely on *istislah* (public advantage). Then we have those who insist on a dogmatic interpretation of holy texts and others who, like Ibn Rushd, eschewed narrow interpretation in favour of deductive reasoning (*al ta'weel*).

Even when it comes to the consumption of alcoholic drinks, we have different opinions. Whereas most jurists interpret the text addressing the subject as banning drinking altogether, others like Abu Hanifa believe the ban applies only to intoxication. He makes his views on the subject clear in the following passage:

> If it gets me thrown into Hell I will not drink it,
> But even if I am thrown into Hell I will not call it sinful.

1. The Roots of Wahhabism

Islam, as well as incorporating various trends, creeds and schools of thought, has had its share of fanatical hardliners through the ages, from its inception up to the present. As early as the first century of the Muslim calendar, Islam has known radical sects which demanded blind adherence to their rigid reading of the articles of faith, side by side with mainstream Islam, whose adherents eschew violence and extremism and do not profess to hold a monopoly on the truth.

The phenomenon began with the emergence of al-Khawarij (the Seceders) in 660 AD – the middle of Islam's first century. They preached a dogmatic interpretation of Scripture and practised a version of excommunication by branding those who did not adopt its teachings as heretics. This was the first such sect, but by no means the last. Throughout the history of Islam the quiet rhythm of religious life was disrupted many times by marginal groups which tried to impose their extremist views on the majority by violent means.[6] Among the earliest such leaders was Hamdan Ibn Qarmat, founder of an extremist Muslim sect established in eastern Arabia towards the end of the ninth century AD who carried away the Black Stone of the Ka'ba, Islam's holiest shrine. The latest is the man hiding in the caves of Wazirstan, Osama bin Laden.

In between these two was Sayyid Qutb, who came up with a theory that will continue to be a wall separating Muslims from the rest of humanity and from any hope of progress until it is torn down. Known as the 'theory of divine dominion', it postulates that mortals are not ruled by mortals but by God. And who, you might well ask, will make God's wishes known to humanity? The answer is, of course, 'We, the *ulamas*'. This is a theory that holds Muslims hostage to a theocracy overtaken by the march of human progress and places them at the mercy of a power structure dominated by a caste of clerics, even though in most Muslim doctrines there is no such thing as a clergy, no intermediaries between Man and God.

As to the farcical notion of men of religion passing themselves off as men of wide learning, which is the English translation of the word *ulama*, a recent incident illustrates just how limited their fund of knowledge really is. In the course of a debate which took place recently, someone asked one of these *ulamas*, the supreme guide of the Muslim Brotherhood in Egypt,[7] whether he knew who Bill Gates was. His reply: 'I don't, and it is not important to know'! This amazing response also shows how insular and isolated from the realities of modern life these self-appointed authorities truly are.

The Muslim Brotherhood is a political religious movement founded by Hassan al-Banna in Isma'iliyya, Egypt, in 1928. The group calls for the reinstitution of Islam and Islamic law as the main pillars upon which all Arab and Muslim societies should be based. The group rejects secular and Western notions in their plan for the administration of Islamic societies. The group set up a well-organized network of independent welfare institutions such as schools and medical clinics, and gained much influence in Egyptian society. During the 1940s, its secret wing was involved in subversive and violent acts against leading political figures and others who were perceived as its enemies. In 1954, Egypt's President Gamal Abdel Nasser banned the group and suppressed it, executing its leader Sayyid Qutb.

The movement resumed its activities in the 1970s under President Anwar Sadat's political liberalization campaign and even published its own journal, though its publication ceased after renewed political suppression in September 1981. Although the movement stresses its peaceful nature and distances itself from more extreme and violent groups, the official ban continues. In spite of this, the movement continues to operate and even takes part in Egyptian elections by presenting its candidates as independents or by forging coalitions with legitimate parties.

It should be stressed that the groups and sects whose members insisted on a literal interpretation of holy texts and laid down strict rules governing all aspects of life were not the norm or mainstream. The main trend was represented in the main Sunni schools (the most important being the Hanafi, Maliki, Shafi'i and Hanbali, and their offshoots, al-Layth and al-Tabari), as well as the Shia, who are split into a number of sects. Within this general trend, prominent proponents of deductive reasoning emerged, like the great jurist Abu Hanifa, as well as uncompromising champions of tradition, such as Ahmed Ibn-Hanbal.

The conservative Ibn-Hanbal served as the bulwark of orthodoxy and tradition against any intellectual endeavor and for a time exerted a considerable hold on the public imagination. His influence eventually waned, but prior to the decline that preceded its recent resurrection in 1744 AD, in his heyday tradition reigned supreme and very little room was left for reason. The two main disciples of Ibn Hanbal were Ibn Taymiyya and Ibn Qaiyim al-Jawziyya who, like their mentor, allowed no scope for reason or independent thinking, but insisted on a dogmatic adherence to the hadiths as authoritative sources of all matters spiritual and temporal, laying down strict guidelines to govern every aspect of daily life.

In addition, the world of Islam was the scene of a battle of ideas between Abu Hamid al-Ghazali (1058–1111, known as Algazel), a strict traditionalist who did not believe the human mind capable of grasping the truth as ordained by God, and Ibn Rushd (Averroes), who championed the primacy of reason. The exponents of these two schools waged a bitter battle in which the first salvo was fired by al-Ghazali with his book, *The Incoherence of the Philosophers* (*Tahafut al-Falasifa*).

Ibn Rushd answered with his brilliant treatise in defence of rationality, *The Incoherence of the Incoherence* (*Tahafut Al Tahafut*). But despite his spirited defence, the outcome of the battle was clearly in al-Ghazali's favour, and the great majority of Islamic jurists adopted his ideas, interpreting the precepts of Islamic law by appeal to the authority of tradition and spurning deductive reasoning altogether. Islamic jurisprudence was dominated by the Mutaqalimun, (dialectical theologians), who asserted the primacy of tradition (*naql*), as advocated by al-Ghazali, over that of reason (*aql*), as advocated by Ibn Rushd.

While the 'worshippers of the word' and 'prisoners of tradition' triumphed, Ibn Rushd's championship of the primacy of reason, though rejected by the Muslim world, took root strongly in Europe, particularly in France, which embraced his vision wholeheartedly. Europe's gain was our loss; as in turning our backs on Ibn Rushd, we lost a historic opportunity for development.

A close reading of Ibn Taymiyya's works, as well as the works of his disciples, from Ibn Qaiyim al-Jawziyya to Muhammad Ibn Abd al-Wahhab at the end of the eighteenth century, deepens one's aversion towards this trend and admiration for the Mu'tazaliyya, who emphasized human responsibility in matters of religion as well as for liberal thinkers who chose the path of reason over that of dogma, like Ibn Sinna, known as Avicenna (980–1037), al-Farabi (870–950), and the leading exponent of this school, Ibn Rushd himself.

Even today, a reader can clearly see that the works of al-Ghazali are indeed distinctly lacking in rationality.[8] In comparison, rationality reigns supreme in the writings of Ibn Rushd.[9] Why, then, did the Muslims give both a victory to al-Ghazali, the proponent of orthodoxy and tradition for whom knowledge meant only knowledge of religion and who rejected the role of the mind altogether by denying the possibility of acquiring knowledge through intuition, and a crushing defeat for Ibn Rushd, who upheld the primacy of reason and sowed the seeds of a renaissance we chose not to reap?

The answer to this paradox can be summed up in one word: despotism. It is amazing how historians of Islamic thought concealed the fact that al-Ghazali was unfailingly supportive of despotic rulers, while Ibn Rushd was a constant source of irritation for tyrants determined to keep their subjects in a state of intellectual inertia, thereby guaranteeing perpetuation of the status quo and their continued, unchallenged authority. For an active mind is the source of questions, and questions lead to accountability. As an enlightened friend put it, questions have eyes and answers are blind!

At a time when despotism in our part of the world was at its height, it is not surprising that Muslim rulers should have found al-Ghazali's ideas more appealing than those of Ibn Rushd. The orthodox line was also more appealing to their subjects who, under the yoke of tyranny, found it safer and less demanding to go along with the views of those who required nothing more from them than a suspension of their critical faculties.

In Europe, where the forces of enlightenment were locked in a confrontation with the clericalism that stifled intellectual initiative and rational thought, despotism was in retreat. This explains why, in the thirteenth century, a prestigious centre of learning like the University of Paris supported the ideas of the Arab Muslim Ibn Rushd over those of the European Christian Thomas Aquinas, the thirteenth-century scholastic philosopher who believed that truth can be known through both reason and faith.

The Muslim world continued to be ruled by despots who

brooked no challenge to their authority and an equally despotic religious establishment that decried the use of reason and demanded blind adherence to the authority of tradition. Closely linked as to methods, motivations and goals, these two factors created an atmosphere that was inimical to the unhindered pursuit of knowledge.

Even so, issues were not simply black or white. True, the Muslims lost a historic opportunity to use Ibn Rushd's ideas as a springboard that could have placed them on a path similar to the one which took Europe from the obscurantist thinking of the thirteenth century to a vigorous intellectual climate encouraging debate, free thinking, general freedoms and creativity in literature, art and science.

But it is also true that Muslims have known both: one interpretation of Islam which allowed for the acceptance of the 'Other'; another that was rigid, doctrinaire, and violently repressing free thought. The first took hold in the more intellectually vibrant climate that prevailed among the peoples descended from ancient civilizations in places like Egypt, Iraq, Turkey and the Levant, which I call the 'Turkish–Egyptian model of Islam'. The second can best be described as the Bedouin model, and was espoused by the secret sects (limited in number and influence) which emerged in remote areas of the Arabian Peninsula together with the rise of Wahhabism, a puritan revival movement launched by Muhammad Ibn Abd al-Wahhab from Najd, in what is now central Saudi Arabia, where he was born in 1703.

Although the first Turkish–Egyptian model of Islam can in no way be described as secular, it adopted an enlightened approach to religion, dealing with it as a system of spiritual beliefs rather than as a system that ruled all aspects of life and governed the affairs of society. Even if it cannot claim to have attained the level of enlightenment, progressive thinking and freedom that characterizes the ideas of Ibn Rushd, it was nevertheless a gentle and tolerant Islam that could and did coexist with others.

The altogether different Bedouin model of Islam was taking shape among geographically isolated communities living far from coastlines and hence from exposure to the outside world. Their insularity provided an ideal breeding ground for the ideas of Ibn Taymiyya, Ibn Qaiyim al-Jawziyya and, toward the end of the eighteenth century, those of Muhammad Ibn Abd al-Wahhab.

This was the mode of thought that produced the Saudi Brotherhood who waged war on King Abd al-Aziz Ibn Saud

(1870–1953) in the 1920s. It has since metamorphosed into a powerful ideology thanks to the combination of the ideas of Sayyid Qutb, petrodollars, and a series of blunders on the part of international, regional and local players. One such blunder was what happened in Afghanistan at the end of the 1970s. Another was the late Egyptian President Anwar Sadat's[10] ill-advised decision to give free rein to Islamic groups and consider them allies in his war on the Left during that decade. Not surprisingly, the move was orchestrated by senior members of the Muslim Brotherhood acting through their mouthpiece, the wealthy businessman and close confidante of Sadat, Usman Ahmad Usman.

2. The Growth of Wahhabism

The man who founded Wahhabism was not a theologian but a proselytizer who was determined to convert the faithful to his harsh brand of Islam. Intellectually close to the dialectical Islamic theologians who asserted the primacy of tradition (*naql*) over reason (*aql*), Muhammad Ibn Abd al-Wahhab was a disciple of Ibn Taymiyya, a strict traditionalist who allowed little scope for reason or independent thinking. He was also a product of his geographical environment, a remote outpost of history.

Unlike Egypt, Syria, Lebanon, Iraq and Yemen, where ancient civilizations had flourished and left their mark on human history, or places like al-Hijaz and a number of the Gulf coastal cities, which lay on trade routes and dealt extensively with the outside world, the desert of Najd in the Eastern Province of what is now Saudi Arabia had no civilization to speak of before Islam. Nor did it ever become a cultural centre like the various capitals of the Caliphate[11] from the seventh to the sixteenth centuries: Medina, Damascus and Baghdad. Thanks to its arid, barren landscape, Najd remained a cultural backwater, its sole contribution to the arts a traditional form of poetry that spoke of narrow tribal matters.

In 1744, Abd al-Wahhab forged an alliance with the ruler of al-Diriyya,[12] a tribal chieftain by the name of Muhammad Ibn Saud, who became his son-in-law. The alliance led to the first incarnation of the Saudi state, which, by 1804, had expanded to control a huge area in the Arabian Peninsula. A collision between the two models of Islam was inevitable, and, in the second decade of the nineteenth century, they confronted one another on the battlefield. Muhammad

Ali,[13] the Egyptian ruler who introduced his country and the region generally to the modern age, sent a huge army to the Arabian Peninsula to destroy the newly established Saudi–Wahabi state governed according to the strict Wahhabi interpretation of Islam.

In 1818, the Egyptian army, and with it, the more enlightened Turkish–Egyptian model of Islam, emerged victorious. They defeated the enemy, destroyed their capital, al-Diriyya, and captured their leader, who was later executed in Istanbul. Muhammad Ali's decision to destroy the first Saudi state had implications going far beyond the political or military ambitions of one man. In fact, it was an expression of a confrontation in terms of culture and civilization between the two forms of Islam.

Muhammad Ali, who was extremely impressed by the European model of development and saw no contradiction between the mechanisms by which it had come about and his own Islamic beliefs, considered that the Wahhabi understanding of Islam stood as a major obstacle in the way of the dream he had nurtured since coming to power in 1805 – and would hold until he abdicated in favour of his son, Ibrahim, in 1848 – to place Egypt on a similar road to development.

Although the moderate, tolerant, mainstream version of Islam, which accepted peaceful coexistence with others and was not pathologically opposed to progress and modernity, emerged victorious in that particular round of its confrontation with the forces of obscurantism, it was later forced to retreat before such internal factors as oppression, absence of social mobility, spread of incompetence, despair, outdated educational systems and corruption.

The winds of change were blowing throughout the region, and the years that followed were not kind to Turkey and Egypt. The collapse of the Ottoman Empire after the First World War brought an end to Turkey's ascendancy, while Egypt's influence receded as its economy and educational system declined. At the same time, the proponents of the model of Islam which demanded a strict adherence to the letter of scripture and slammed the door shut in the face of rationality suddenly found themselves, in the mid-twentieth century, in control of vast wealth unprecedented in history. This gave the Saudis an enormous edge over their moderate rivals and allowed them to extend their influence into the traditional strongholds of the Turkish–Egyptian model of Islam, where they waged a systematic campaign to co-opt establishment personalities and institutions.

The success of this campaign found its most salient expression in the emergence of fanatical movements like the Taliban in Afghanistan. Thus that other, stricter version of Islam found opportunities to spread its uncompromising message to every corner of the world for the first time, aided by international conditions – and lack of vision – which allowed what had once been an obscure sect confined behind the sand dunes of Najd to impose itself on the world stage and boldly proclaim its brand of Islam as the one and only 'true Islam'.

As the drama played out, some of the spectators chose to look the other way because the sword-wielding hero of the piece, Osama bin Laden, was playing the role required of him at the time by fighting the Soviets in Afghanistan. Thus they failed to realize that the hero was no longer sticking to the script set for him but was now playing a much more central and dangerous role. This unfortunate state of affairs could have been avoided if the majority of Muslims had supported Ibn Rushd's ideas or if conditions had not forced the retreat of the Turkish–Egyptian model.

The harsh and unforgiving environment in which the Najdis lived explains why Muhammad Ibn Abd al-Wahhab found a receptive audience for the equally harsh and unforgiving brand of Islam he preached. The same environment that produced the founder of Wahhabism later produced the radical Ikhwan movement which challenged the authority of King Abd al-Aziz Ibn Saud. In the 1920s, the king took on the Ikhwan, who were openly accusing him of deviating from the true faith.

They waged a conflict over any of the fruits of modernity which threatened their fundamentalist vision of the world. Among other things, they banned tombstones and any structures identifying burial sites, insisting on unmarked graves that lay flush with the ground. They combated Sufism, a mystically oriented interpretation of Islam, as contrary to the teachings of Islam.

The Ikhwan even staged an armed attack on the Egyptian *mahmal*, a splendidly decorated litter on which the Egyptians sent a new cover for the Ka'ba every year. The *mahmal* ceremony was a festive occasion celebrated by the Egyptians with their traditional love of music, dancing and revelry. For the Najdis, who had launched their puritanical revival movement to purge Islam of what they saw as deviations from the straight and true path of orthodoxy, such unseemly displays of levity could not be tolerated.

While the desert wasteland of the Arabian Peninsula's Eastern Province had suffered greatly from its geography throughout history, in modern times it was found to contain the richest oil fields. The resulting wealth intensified by the oil price boom beginning in the 1970s turned the desert kingdom into a major financial power. It was inevitable that this part of the world should try and market its ideas. This it did with missionary zeal in the second half of the twentieth century.

With a virtually endless supply of funds at their disposal, the Wahhabis were able to successfully propagate their model of Islam throughout the Arab and Muslim world. Disillusioned populations, facing massive internal problems caused by political oppression and its consequences were easy prey, and mainstream Islam gradually lost ground to the austere, puritanical Wahhabi model that was now presenting itself as the one and only true Islam.

3. Flawed Education

Educational systems that are out of step with the age are a vital link in this chain of destruction. Educational systems in most Islamic and Arab societies encourage insularity and reinforce a sense of isolation from the rest of humanity, promote fanaticism and lay down, without any scientific basis, religious frameworks for struggles that are purely political. By invoking religious texts taken out of context they not only promote intolerance, non-acceptance of the 'Other', and a lack of belief in pluralism, but also consecrate the lowly status of women.

Moreover, most of the curricula are designed to develop a mentality of 'answering' rather than of 'questioning', in a world where progress and development are driven by the dynamics of posing questions. In most Islamic and Arab societies, educational programmes fail to instil in the minds of the young the idea that 'progress' is a human process, in the sense that its mechanisms are neither eastern nor western, but universal. This is borne out by the fact that the list of most advanced countries in the world includes some that are Western/Christian, like the United States and western Europe, and others that are Japanese, Chinese or even have a Muslim background, such as Malaysia.

There is a clear and growing tendency in the humanities and social sciences to disengage, as it were, from the common fund of human experience, the cumulative legacy built up over the ages by various civilizations. For many in past generations, for example those born in the 1940s and 1950s, there was the opportunity to read the classics of world literature and thought in Arabic. Writers such as Aeschylus, Aristophanes, Euripides, Sophocles, Virgil, Dante, Shakespeare, Racine, Molière, Voltaire, Jean-Jacques Rousseau, all the Russian classics, Flaubert, Balzac, Bernard Shaw, Homer, Jean-Paul Sartre, Pirandello, Albert Camus, John Steinbeck, William Faulkner, and the gems of German philosophy were translated by people predominantly from Egypt, Syria and Lebanon, and published mainly in Egypt and Lebanon.

Being able to read these timeless classics of world literature – without being told that to do so was somehow 'un-Muslim' or disloyal, linked many such intellectuals to humanity in a way that is inconceivable today. The number of such translations has also fallen in the cultural milieu in Arab and Islamic countries; the distance between the minds of young people in contemporary Islamic and Arab societies and the masterpieces of human creativity has increased dramatically. The new generations have become increasingly 'local', setting themselves still further apart from humanity and increasing the mentality of violence and its culture.

4. Religious Teaching in Egypt

Between 16 and 25 per cent, depending on the source, of those enrolled in the Egyptian educational system today are studying in religious educational establishments, schools, academies and colleges run by al-Azhar, the central Islamic institution of higher education. This amounts to between three and five million young people receiving their education from start to finish in religious institutions, and this educational phenomenon is bound to have far-reaching social, political and economic ramifications.

First, why does a society like Egypt's end up sending such large numbers of its youth to study at religious schools? Was it planned or is it a random development that grew out of a reality not governed by strategic planning but by arbitrary decisions and bureaucracy? Apart from Saudi Arabia, Iran, Afghanistan, Pakistan, Sudan and Yemen, no similar phenomenon exists in any other of the more than 200 states in the world. Accordingly, did this situation arise because Egyptians do not aspire to be more like Japan, Singapore, France,

Canada or Spain (educationally and hence culturally) than like Saudi Arabia, Iran, Afghanistan, Pakistan, Sudan and Yemen? And is this what Egyptians aimed for when they laid down a strategic educational policy in full awareness of its implications and consequences? It beggars belief that they could knowingly have put in place an educational policy aimed at having so many young people enrolled in the educational system receive their education in religious establishments. In fact, the country never set such a policy or, indeed, any educational policy at all!

This situation arose as a result of realities on the ground as well as bureaucracy. The huge number of educational religious establishments sprouted up haphazardly in reaction to specific problems, such as the lack of educational institutions within easy reach of children living in small towns and villages and as a place of educational refuge for pupils who could not, whether for lack of material means or minimal educational requirements, join the general education system.

It is alarming that the establishment of this network of religious schools was the easiest solution to the difficulties in educating the lowest social classes and the segments of society with the poorest learning skills. If so, this means that from a strategic point of view huge numbers of the most disadvantaged elements of society – economically, socially and in terms of learning skills – are being funnelled into a religious educational system without making any effort to consider the strategic results – political, economic and social – of this 'solution' for the future of society.

When questioned as to whether their children were attending al-Azhar schools, the great majority of people who have some minimal means replied in the negative and expressed disdain for the quality of education provided by these schools. This would make it seem that religious education is also perceived as the last refuge of those who, for lack of social, economic or intellectual abilities, have no recourse to the general education system. Allowing this phenomenon to flourish unchecked will have dire consequences for society at large.

Over the last few decades, Egyptian society has been swept by a powerful wave of obscurantism, as evidenced by the primitive and archaic understanding of religion that has become all too prevalent. And yet no one seems to have studied the relationship between this wave and the hordes of mainly underprivileged members of society who have studied in religious educational establishments and who are, for obvious reasons, particularly vulnerable to the appeal of a simplistic understanding of religion.

Have any of our strategic thinkers examined the phenomenon from another angle and asked themselves what effect these huge numbers of Egyptian students enrolled in religious establishments will have on the country's scientific, technological, industrial and trade sectors? Will this have an impact, as it has in other countries which expanded religious education to the point which gave rise to a cadre of men of religion determined to prevent their societies from joining the march of progress?

The values of progress are a set forming an integral part of the ethos of every prosperous society. Among the most important of these are belief in human diversity, pluralism, the universality of knowledge, human rights and women's rights. To review the curricula offered by al-Azhar's educational establishments on various subjects such as culture, literature and languages finds them to be either totally devoid of any attempt to plant the seeds of these values in their students' minds or actively promoting opposing values. To produce graduates whose conscience and mentality are inculcated with values diametrically opposed to the values of progress is going to have a devastatingly negative impact on Egypt.

Allowing such a huge number of religious educational establishments to mushroom ultimately serves a trend that has rightfully been described by the state as the worst enemy of civil society. Is the society and state financing the enemies of civil society and of progress?

5. Absence of 'Competence'

Over the last four decades, many have written about the phenomenon of rising violence in a large number of Islamic and Arab societies. Strangely enough, none of those who wrote used the terms 'competent' or 'incompetent' in their analysis of this phenomenon.[14] Yet the despair felt by so many in Islamic and Arab societies, the sense of helplessness and hopelessness that breeds anger and then violence, stems from the fact that these societies are run by people selected not for their competence but for their subservience and allegiance. After all, competence, as defined by modern management science, is of no great concern to an autocratic political system.

The Example of Egypt

The roots of religious extremism in Egypt stem from three sources. The first is the harsh treatment meted out to the followers of the Islamic trend in Egypt by Nasser's regime in the 1950s and 1960s.[15] Disputes between the regime and the Muslim Brotherhood erupted into serious conflict, and the regime resorted to force and torture against the movement members. The methods used by Nasser against the Islamic political forces – whose members were persecuted, imprisoned, exiled and tortured – created generations of extremists among those who had suffered at his hands. Had they not been trampled upon so harshly by Nasser, the Muslim Brothers would most likely not have produced elements as extremist, as reactionary and as insular as the contemporary militant Islamic groups. The repression of ideas and beliefs produces unexpected forms of extremism, violence, terrorism and even crime. In Egypt the many years of repressive dictatorship also generated a climate of extremism where it had never previously existed.

The second source of extremism in Egypt today is the prevailing socio-economic situation. Many factors combine to create the perfect climate for extremism and the spread of totalitarian tendencies, whether towards the left into Marxist groups or towards the right into sectarianism and religious dogmatism. These factors are: poverty, the decline in living standards, the appearance of a very wealthy minority noted for its conspicuous consumption, the harrowing problems of daily life and the social anarchy they create, as well as a breakdown in society's system of values, the cornerstone on which the system is built.

Karl Marx's[16] famous appeal to the working class, 'Workers of the world unite! You have nothing to lose but your chains!' well illustrates the link between extremism and impecunious socio-economic conditions. Economic crises generate feelings of deep frustration, especially among the young, who despair of attaining their legitimate right to a decent life. The lack of access to such basic necessities as a home, food and clothes and education make them susceptible to hardliners who claim that society is corrupt and doomed and that it should be destroyed to make room for a better one. These disenchanted youngsters were never given the tools to compare their society, whatever its shortcomings, to the insubstantial dream they are offered. Thus the crushing economic crisis and the ensuing breakdown in social values provide an excellent opportunity for advocates of extremism, whether communists or militant religious elements, to peddle their ideas. Finding real solutions to the social and economic difficulties besetting Egypt would certainly help extirpate some of these problems by reducing the appeal of extremism.

The third source can be attributed to external factors. Egypt is in the eye of a storm of radicalism blowing from every direction in the Middle East, especially from Iran and Lebanon, and the contagion is helped along with foreign funding and incitement. The protection of Egyptian society from the scourge of foreign intervention and financing is, of course, the task of the security forces. But as important as this is, their role in dealing with the phenomenon of religious fanaticism cannot eliminate its causes nor bring it to a halt.

The only effective cure is a combination of real democracy (as opposed to window dressing) and firm action by eminent religious figures who should use their moral authority to contain the problem, not fan the flames of extremism as so many do. Last but not least, the vigilance of the security forces is needed, particularly in Upper Egypt where traditional tribal values combined with religious fanaticism constitute a highly explosive mixture.

II. 'THE CLASH OF CIVILIZATIONS' – TRUE OR FALSE?

The mentality of violence produced by internal factors is thus a variable that has emerged only in the last four decades. Its inclusion as a constant in the 'clash of civilizations' paradigm is not only forced but also belongs more to the realm of science fiction than political analysis, for example as in the notorious book by Samuel P. Huntington, whose theory is closely linked to the issue of the mentality of violence. It was first published as an article in 1993 under the title 'The Clash of Civilizations?'[17] and it was then expanded into a book and published the following year under the same title – but without the question mark.[18] The book was a publishing event, selling more copies and provoking more controversy than any other non-fiction book that year.

The main flaw of Huntingdon's book is that the author talks of Islam as a monolith, as though the Wahhabi model is the only version of Islam. Mainstream Islam, however, was quite distinct from the Wahhabi interpretation of Islam and its culture. The only relationship between the Ottoman Empire, which represented Islam politically as a superpower for several centuries, and Wahhabism was one of extreme animosity. If Huntington had used the term 'Wahhabi Islam', his thesis would have made more sense.

Another flaw is that he did not present any evidence to support his theory of an impending clash between the West and what he calls 'Confucian'[19] societies, making the theory closer to fiction, specifically to the writings of H.G. Wells,[20] than to political analysis. It also owes much to Noam Chomsky's[21] equally unfounded theory that the United States needs an enemy to survive, and that this role was filled by the Eastern Bloc from 1945 to 1990. Following the collapse of communism, Chomsky believes that Islam is now the prime candidate for the role! But if so, how can one explain the enormous progress made by the United States between 1500 and 1900, without any external conflicts and without any clear enemy during this period of the development and completion of the American Dream? How can one explain that despite Winston Churchill's[22] efforts from 1939 to 1941 to convince the United States to join the war on the side of the Allies, it was only after the Japanese attack on Pearl Harbour in 1941 that his efforts were crowned with success? How could the United States have resisted the opportunity to benefit from the existence of a ready-made enemy which, according to Chomsky, it needed for its very survival?

A third flaw is that Huntingdon did not devote enough space in his book to the largest conflict in the history of humanity, namely the Second World War, which was fought between forces belonging to the same Western civilization. It was also a conflict within the Christian world; however, nobody ever mentioned religion as a factor in this huge conflict, which was primarily a conflict between European Fascism and European democracies.

To disprove the allegation that the violent groups who turn their backs on modernity and call for a return to the Middle Ages are the true representatives of Islam, one has only to consider how some of the principal Islamic societies were functioning at the turn of the twentieth century. Countries like Egypt, Greater Syria[23](which included Lebanon at the time) and Turkey were models of tolerance, their majority Muslim populations living peacefully with minorities of other faiths. Renowned cosmopolitan cities such as Alexandria, Beirut and Cairo were home to a wide diversity of minorities. Acceptance of the 'Other' and of modernity, as well as a hunger for the great masterpieces of human creativity, were features shared by all these societies.

Although these societies were in complete harmony with the scientific, philosophical and artistic consequences of the Renaissance, they retained their national identity as Egyptians, Turks and Syrians. It was a time when Muslims saw no contradiction between their religious faith and their enthusiasm for the material and cultural fruits of European civilization. Under non-Wahhabi Islam the Muslim communities in Egypt, Syria, Lebanon and Turkey were forward-looking, in tune with the times and living in harmony with large Christian and Jewish communities. It is inconceivable that Wahhabism would have tolerated the kind of cosmopolitan and broad-minded societies that flourished in Alexandria, Cairo, Istanbul, Beirut, Damascus and Aleppo at the turn of the twentieth century. On the contrary, the Najdi version of Islam exhorts its followers to remain in a constant confrontation with others, with the age, and with modernity.

Under Wahhabism, the word *jihad* is interpreted as the need to carry a sword at all times; yet mainstream Islam for centuries understood this word as requiring Muslims to resort to force only to defend themselves against outside aggression. Even semantically, the word *jihad* is totally unrelated to the notion of armed violence; it stems from the root '*juhd*', and has the Arabic verb '*yajtahid*', which means something between 'to try hard' and 'to struggle'.

Mainstream Islam also accepted the possibility of Muslims merging with the rest of humanity (especially before the chauvinistic tribal culture of Najd gained ground), while Wahhabism regards this as not possible and unacceptable. Indeed, it is regarded as synonymous with subservience, a term that is widely used by those whose thinking is shaped by the Wahhabi model of Islam.

The peaceful and harmonious coexistence of devout Muslims with the religious minorities living in their midst, and their equally harmonious relationship with the fruits of Western civilization proves conclusively that the adherents of 'real' Islam are not violent fanatics and that mainstream Islam has nothing to do with the Wahhabi model of militant Islam, whose success in winning over converts is due to the declining and depressing conditions in many Islamic societies. The Islamic system of belief does not lead inevitably to violence and clashes with the 'Other'.

Violence and fanaticism are features of only one fringe sect virtually unknown outside the deserts of Najd as recently as one century ago. Non-Wahhabi mainstream Islam prevailed in Islamic societies until two cataclysmic developments forced it to retreat: first, the eruption of the violent model of Islam from behind the sand dunes; second, the decline in living standards in many Islamic societies which allowed it to spread.

III. EXTERNAL FACTORS

While the mentality of violence is caused primarily by internal factors, an external factor contributed to its spread, namely, the misguided attempts by some to use the forces produced by the mentality of violence for political purposes. A case in point is the support to the Saud family by British intelligence after the First World War, helping create there a political system deriving its legitimacy from a Wahhabi interpretation of Islam at the beginning of the twentieth century. The Najdi movement, known as the Ikhwan or brotherhood, was a prime example of this trend. King Abd al-Aziz Ibn Saud was forced to go to war against them in the 1920s after they accused him of deviating from the tenets of what they interpreted as being 'real' Islam, by accepting such western abominations as radios, cars, telephones, etc.

During the same period, Egypt saw an alliance formed between the British and the monarchy, where both had an interest in creating a political entity deriving its attractiveness from the popularity of religion in Egypt to counterbalance the influential Wafd Party,[24] which spearheaded the Egyptian struggle for a constitution, parliament and independence. Forged in secret, the alliance is now known to anyone studying Egypt's modern history.

A third example of the dangerous game politicians play with the mentality of violence in the hope that they can use it to further their own ends was the US promotion in Afghanistan of radical Islamic groups against the USSR. Had it not been for the Cold War and for the short-sighted belief by some that religion could be used as a winning card in the confrontation, the mentality of violence could never have reached its present alarming proportions.

Thus although it is largely a product of internal factors, the mentality of violence was given a huge boost by the unlimited petrodollar wealth – let alone the enormous US mistake which can be described as the greatest miscalculation of the Cold War era: the use of political Islam to counteract communism.

Thus the world, having rid itself of Fascism, Nazism and then

Communism, now finds itself locked in yet another confrontation, this time with a brand of militant political Islam resulting from a shift in the centre of gravity in the Muslim world – its migration from Egypt to nomadic Arabia.

The assassination of President Anwar Sadat in 1981 by an extremist group was a wake-up call alerting the world to the growth and spread of the Saudi-backed Wahhabi form of Islam and the retreat of the Turkish–Egyptian model. A succession of similar events attested to the dangerous spread of this model in most societies with a Muslim majority, such as Nigeria, Algeria, Egypt, the Arabian Peninsula, Pakistan, Afghanistan and Indonesia.

On the morning of 11 September 2001 a group of fanatics following the Wahhabi brand of Islam launched attacks on New York and Washington that illustrated how the members of this sect view the 'Other' in general, and Western civilization in particular.

IV. PROGRESS AND MODERNITY OBSTRUCTED

During the first five hundred years of their religion, Muslims witnessed enormous intellectual developments across a broad range of subjects in Islamic thinking, including the fundamentals of jurisprudence, linguistics, interpretation and historiography. These intellectual advances resulted in a revolution of opinions and interpretations that varied from the extreme right – such as the Hanbali school – to the utmost level of reason-based interpretation proposed by the great thinker Ibn Rushd (Averroes).

Between those two extremes were a multitude of other schools of thought. However, a combination of closed autocratic regimes, outdated educational systems, state-controlled media, and a rigid, often extremist, understanding of religion rendered many Muslims and Arabs wary of notions like 'progress' and 'modernity'. Both internal factors and some external ones have led the Muslim Arab mind to think that the call for progress and modernity is one for dependence on the West, and hence the loss of cultural specificity.

What exacerbates the situation is that many Arabs and Muslims feel that the values of Western civilization are for Westerners only, and not for everyone. In fact, modernization is above all a phenomenon common to all humanity. The prescription for progress has no nationality or religion, as borne out by the different cultural backgrounds of such developed societies as the United States, Japan, Malaysia, Taiwan and South Korea.

The difference between successful and unsuccessful societies does not differ across national lines. Japan rapidly developed along lines almost precisely the same as those of the West but remains distinctly Japanese. Whoever denies that progress is a purely human phenomenon and that the process leading to it is also human has never seen the mechanics of progress at first hand.

Yet oppressive regimes want to persuade their people that modernity requires dependence and a loss of national and religious identity. Citizens who lack a broad education and are cut off from the outside world are likely to agree with this idea. They would be inclined to consider democracy not as a human right but as a system conceived in the West that was appropriate only for Westerners. Similarly, they would believe that their own society, identity and beliefs are unsuited for democracy. Yet even though there are many forms of democracy they all have in common the existence of mechanisms which force the rulers to account to the people; this makes governments the servants rather than the masters of society.

Muslims committed a grave mistake against themselves and their religion when they closed the door to *ijtihad* (interpretation by reasoning) and stopped searching for new concepts and solutions. They became satisfied with simply emulating and reiterating what their ancestors had produced, although those concepts and solutions were the outcome of an ancient era. Therefore, Muslims are living in a static, unchanging environment where they ruminate on the thoughts of other men who exerted themselves to formulate concepts that suited their time eight centuries ago.

In contrast to ancient Muslim men of religion such as Ibn Rushd (Averroes), who is as important intellectually as Aristotle, contemporary Muslim scholars tend to use only Arabic sources, are not aware of modern sciences, and find themselves in social environments that prevent them from being intellectually open to the innovations of humanity in the different fields of social and human sciences.

A. Scholars

Thus the Arabic-speaking world is in dire need of a new generation of scholars who can comprehend the sciences, cultures and knowledge of the current age as well as understand the heritage of early Muslims. Seventy years ago, the grand imam of al-Azhar, Dr

Mustafa Abd al-Raziq, was a professor of philosophy in a university, not the University of al-Riyadh or the University of Sana'a, but the Sorbonne.[25]

Why is it that the Vatican abounds with men of religion with such splendid educational, intellectual, and encyclopaedic cognitive backgrounds in their various areas of knowledge, while Muslim scholars hardly know anything about the great fruits of human creativity in many of the different branches of social and human sciences! Consider Yusuf al-Qaradawi, the man seen by many as the greatest Muslim jurist and preacher of his time. He was an Egyptian with Qatari nationality who fled from Egypt during the clashes between the Muslim Brotherhood and Gamal Abdel Nasser in 1954. He could only participate in international conferences through an interpreter and never became involved in discussions about modern thought. In comparison, the Vatican scholars present used multiple languages and showed that they commanded vast fields of knowledge. The gap was enormous.

What is needed then is a generation of Muslim religious scholars who have studied other religions, human history, world literature, philosophy, sociology and psychology and can speak several languages. Collectively, this constitutes the language of civilization. Until this happens, Muslim scholars will remain at their level of naivety, shallowness and isolation from the path of civilization and humanity.

Just as Muslims are underdeveloped in all fields of science, they also have not advanced in the study of their own religion. Their backwardness in Islam is the same as it is in medicine, engineering, information technology and space research. Thus the gap between Muslims and the progress of humanity will increase. Campaigns of criticism will escalate against them; clashes between Islam and the West may reoccur. Muslims (or to be more precise, large sectors of the Muslim population) will become the primary enemy of Western civilization or may even become the leading enemy of humanity at large.

B. Institutions

Despite this dire need, such development within Islamic religious institutions is very unlikely to occur. The largest Islamic institutions in the modern world, especially in Saudi Arabia and Egypt, expel anyone calling for the slightest reform or change. If so, then what should we expect when demands for comprehensive changes are voiced? A prominent Islamic university dismissed Dr Ahmad Subhi Mansur[26] for his rejection of prophetic hadiths as a source of jurisprudential principles. The university should have discussed the differences in viewpoints using a scientific method that would be performed within the framework of a dialogue, and organized debates for differing scholars to exchange opinions.

Strangely enough, Abu Hanifa al-Nu'man, one of the four great Muslim jurists many centuries ago found himself in the same situation as Mansur when he decided to recognize only a few of the prophetic hadiths at a time when other jurists accepted all of them. If Abu Hanifa had seen a book like *Sahih al-Bukhari*,[27] the most trusted collection of hadiths today, he would have rejected more than 90 per cent of its contents. In this situation some modern Islamic universities would have deemed Abu Hanifa a *kafir* (unbeliever) although he was the first of the four great Islamic jurists and was given the title of 'The Great Imam'.[28]

Conditions in today's Islamic religious institutions do not allow those institutions to produce men of the quality of Abu Hanifa and Averroes. They are more and more isolated and occupied with religious references that have become brittle with age. For centuries, their role in the interpretation of Islam has been restricted to the texts of books and not their contexts. It has become rare to find any scholars in Muslim universities who have read even one book in a language other than Arabic.

The long-sought for change among the Islamic establishment is now contingent upon a political leadership willing to lean toward a rational interpretation of history and a vision for the future. Unfortunately, these qualifications are not easily found within Islamic communities. Nevertheless, we must demand a political leadership that would work toward achieving radical procedural change within the structure of the Islamic scholarly community, one willing to bring this community in harmony with the age of science and the progress of humanity. Without this driving force, Muslims will be heading for a massive confrontation with humanity which will be as disastrous as a collision between two celestial bodies.

NOTES

1. Leading intellectual of the Egyptian Muslim Brotherhood.
2. 1937–2006. President of Iraq from 1979 to 2003; sentenced to death and hanged by an

Iraqi government installed by US authority, and tried on a specimen charge of executing 148 Shiites suspected of planning his assassination.

3. Abu Ja'far Muhammad ibn Jarir Al-Tabari (838–923 AD). Persian historian, author of *Tarikh al Rusul wal Mulūk* [History of the Prophets and Kings] (Albany, NY: The State University of New York Press, 1985–2007), and *Jāmiʿ al-bayān ʿan taʾwīl āy al-Qurʾān* [The commentary on the Quran] (Cairo: 1902/03).
4. Imam Laith Ibn-Saad (94–175 AH). Sunni Muslim Jurist and sheikh (clergyman) of Imam Malik; lived in Egypt, see Mohamed Rawas Kalmagy, *Mawsuʿat fiqh al Laith ibn Saʿd* [Encyclopedia of Al Laith ibn Saad's Islamic Jurisprudence] (Kuwait: Kuwait University, Majlis al Nashr al 'Ilmy, 2002).
5. Famous saying by the fourth Caliph Ali Ibn-Abi Talib who was murdered near the city of Najaf (Iraq) in 661 AD. See Al Sharif al Radi Abi al Hassan Mohamed ibn al Hussayn ibn Mussa ibn Mohamed ibn Mussa ibn Ibrahim ibn al Imam Mussa al Qaddhim, *Nahj-ul-balagha*, [Peak of Eloquence] (Letter 77, p.624), available at http://aqaed.info/ pdf/shial-ib/498.pdf.
6. A comprehensive history of these groups has been compiled by Professor Mahmoud Ismail Abdul Razzak, in an authoritative reference work titled *The Secret Sects in Islam* (*Al haraqāt al sirriyah fil islām)*, 5th edn, (Cairo and Beirut: Sina Lel Nashr and Mu'assassat al Intishar al 'Arabi, 1997). The author devotes special attention to the Qarmatians, who carried away the Black Stone of the Ka'ba and kept it in a remote area in the east of the Arabian Peninsula for over a century.
7. The Muslim Brotherhood is a political religious movement founded by Hassan Al-Banna in Ismailia, Egypt, in 1928. The group calls for the reinstitution of Islam and Islamic law as the main pillars upon which the Egyptian – indeed, all Arab and Muslim societies – should be based. The group rejects secular and Western notions for the governance of Islamic societies. As part of their Islamic notions the group set up a well-organized network of independent welfare institutions such as schools and medical clinics, and gained much influence in Egyptian society. During the 1940s, its secret wing was involved in subversive and violent acts against leading political figures and others who were perceived as its enemies. In 1954, Gamal Abdel Nasser banned the group and suppressed it, executing its leader, Sayed Qutb. The movement resumed its activities in the 1970s under Sadat's political liberalization, and even published its own journal, though publication ceased after renewed political suppression in September 1981. Although the movement stresses its peaceful nature and distances itself from more extreme and violent groups, the official ban on it continues. In spite of this, the movement continues to operate and even takes part in Egyptian elections by presenting its candidates as independents or by forging coalitions with legitimate parties.
8. For example, *The Revival of the Religious Sciences* [*Ihya' Ulum ad-Din*] (Cambridge: Islamic Texts Society, 1990), *The Criterion of Knowledge* [*Mi'yar al-'Elm*] (Cairo: al-Maṭbaʻah al-ʻArabīyah, 1927), *The Balance of Work* [*Mizan al-'Amal*] (Lebanon: Dar al Kotob Al-ilmiyah, 2000), *Salvation From Perdition* [*Al-Monqedh Min al'Dallal*] (Beirut: al-Lajnah al-Duwalīyah li-Tarjamat al-Rawāʼiʻ, 1959), *The Essence of Orthodoxy* [*Al-Mustafa Min Elm al-Osoul*] (Beirut: Mu'assasat al-Risālah, 1997), and *The Incoherence of the Philosophers* [*Tahafut al-Falasifah*], first published in the eleventh century, available at http://www.ghazali.org/works/taf-eng.pdf.
9. Including *The Distinguished Jurist's Primer* (*Bidayat al-Mujtahid Wa Nihayat al-Muqtasid*) (selections in English) (Leyden: Brill, 1977), *Relationship of Religious Law with Philosophy* [*Fasl al-Maqal fi ma bayn al-Shari'a wa al-hikma min al-Ittisal*] (Cairo: Dār al-Maʻārif , 1972), and *Islamic Doctrine and Its Proofs* [*Al-Kashf 'an Manahij al-Adilla fi 'Aqa'id al-Milla*] (Egypt: al-Maktabah Maḥmūdīyah al-Tijārīyah, 1935).
10. 1918–1981. Egyptian President from 1970 to 1981. Graduated from the Military Academy in 1938. Expelled from the army and imprisoned in 1940s for subversive political activities and suspicion of participation in plots to assassinate senior political figures. When he was released, he rejoined the armed forces in 1950. He took part in the 1952 Free Officers Revolution and was a close ally of Gamal Abdel Nasser, who appointed Sadat in 1969 as his vice-president. When Nasser died, in September 1970, Sadat succeeded him as president. During the first years of his presidency Sadat quelled leftist opposition, surprised Israel in what was considered the victory of the 1973 war, reoriented Egyptian

foreign policy towards the West (especially towards the USA), reversing its long pro-Soviet inclination. He introduced a series of economic and political reforms, promoting liberalization. In 1977, in a dramatic act and as a gesture demonstrating his will for peace, Sadat flew to Jerusalem and addressed the Israeli Knesset (parliament). The culmination of the process initiated by his visit was the signing of an Egyptian-Israeli peace agreement at Camp David. In his last years in power, Sadat's rule suffered from growing disillusionment and opposition (mainly from Islamic elements), manifested in the popular riots that broke out in 1977 and his assassination, during a victory parade, on 6 October 1981 by Islamic militants belonging to the Jihad group.

11. Islamic government, the head of the state is the Caliph.
12. It became the Saudi capital from 1744 to 1818 AD.
13. Circa 1769–1849. Governor of Egypt; founder of modern Egypt and of the dynasty which ruled Egypt until the expulsion of King Farouk on 26 July 1952, followed by the abolition of the monarchy on 18 June 1953.
14. This is as true of eminent professors in top-notch universities, like Harvard's Samuel P. Huntington, and Francis Fukuyama as it is of the media, which has taken up the concept and used – if not abused – this 'Huntingtonian' concept and turned it more or less into a slogan.
15. Gamal Abdel Nasser (1918–1970). Second Egyptian President 1954–1970. Graduated from the Military Academy in 1938. Participated as battalion commander in the 1948 War between the Arabs and the fledging State of Israel. After the war, he organized the Free Officers group, which consisted mainly of low-ranking officers, largely from humble backgrounds, whose objective was to revamp what was believed to be a corrupt system, which also implied the overthrow of the royal dynasty then ruling. On 23 July 1952 they successfully executed a coup. Initially the officers installed the coup leader, General Mohamed Naguib, as president. After growing dissent and rivalry, Nasser ousted Naguib and became the official president in 1954. During his presidency Egypt underwent a series of economic, social and political reforms. He banned all parties except his own Arab Socialist Union. In the economic sphere he pursued a socialist policy, in 1961 nationalizing all major industries and utilities and adopting an ambitious development plan, with the project of the Great Dam of Aswan being one of his main achievements. His regime also carried out agrarian reform, redistributing agrarian lands in Egypt. In the international and inter-Arab sphere he adopted a nationalistic revolutionary Arab policy and was one of the co-founders of the non-aligned bloc in 1955. During his time in office Egypt's foreign policy tilted towards the Soviet Union and the Eastern bloc. Some of his most salient actions in the international arena were the nationalization of the Suez Canal in 1956, the union with Syria, the Egyptian involvement in Yemen and the 1967 War after which he resigned for twenty-four hours, only to be reinstated following popular clamour. After his death, Nasser was succeeded by Anwar Al-Sadat.
16. 1818–1883. Prussian revolutionary philosopher and political economist, author of the *Communist Manifesto* (1848).
17. Samuel Huntington, 'The Clash of Civilizations?' *Foreign Affairs* (Summer 1993).
18. Samuel Huntington, *The Clash of Civilizations and the Remaking of World Order* (New York: Simon and Schuster, 1996).
19. Related to the teachings of Confucius, the Chinese philosopher (551–479 BC).
20. 1866–1946. English writer.
21. Born in Philadelphia, 1928. American professor of linguistics and radical political commentator, he describes himself as a 'libertarian anarchist'.
22. British prime minister, 1940 to 1945 and 1951 to 1955.
23. A region in the Middle-East, historically understood to extend from the east of the Mediterranean Sea to the Levant.
24. Political party founded in Egypt by Saad Zaghloul in 1919.
25. Université de Paris II, one of the oldest and most important universities in France, indeed the entire world.
26. Former university professor, liberal Sunni Muslim.
27. Translation of Sahih Bukhari available at http://www.holyebooks.org/islam/hadith_of_bukhari/index.html.
28. An imam is an Islamic leader.

2

Facing the Emergence

For the average European or American unfamiliar with some of the facts presented above, it is easy to believe that Islam, violence, and terrorism go hand in hand. The perception of Islam today by many non-Muslims is that it is a fanatical and violent religion. This is a superficial perception, as it ignores the fact that there are at least two models of Islam: one, uncompromising and extremist in its views; another, tolerant, moderate and humanistic. It is also a naïve perception which can lead to dangerous decisions like the ones made regarding the West's policies, when it turned a blind eye to the spread of Wahhabism and established close links with radical Islamic movements like the Taliban in Afghanistan.

But those who have a more thorough grasp of the issue know that the perception of Islam as uncompromising has taken hold only because a puritanical, fundamentalist model of Islam, marginal and ineffectual before the oil wealth of petrodollars put it on the map, has managed to make the world believe that its interpretation of Islam is the only version and the 'true' Islam.

The doctrinaire version of Islam propounded by the Wahhabis, however, had no followers among the Muslims of the world before the expansion of Saudi influence following the oil boom. Millions of Muslims in Egypt, Turkey, the Levant, Iraq, Indonesia, and throughout the world remained immune to the appeal of the fanatical, violent and bloody message of what was a small and obscure sect bred in the intellectually barren landscape of the eastern Arabian Peninsula.

All that changed with two factors, first and foremost, the massive influx of petrodollars into the coffers of Saudi Arabia, which used its new-found wealth to propagate the message of its home-grown Wahhabi sect with missionary zeal. Hence, militant Islam as a force to be reckoned with on the world stage, a force that now represents a dangerous threat to world peace, to humanity, and equally to Islam and Muslims, emerged.

Second, following the decline in living standards they have suffered since at the hands of despotic and corrupt rulers, many people have become easy prey for the Wahhabi interpretation of Islam along with its counterparts, Qutb's view of Sunni Islam, and virulent Shiite schools.

For example, Egypt, beginning in the 1960s, suffered a reversal of fortune at all levels, including a decline in its general cultural climate, allowing Wahhabi influence to infiltrate al-Azhar, the central Islamic institution of higher education. The defeat of June 1967 opened the door wide to groups which espoused the Saudi understanding of Islam and who translated their radical views into political action, often at gunpoint. These factors start with autocracy, creating a mentality of violence, leading to lack of competence, declining living standards, despair and the collapse of educational systems.

The contemporary situation of Islam, then, is no permanent social phenomenon but the result of circumstances and factors. Yet there is a legitimate reason to fear that non-Wahhabi Islam, the main trend among the majority of Muslims for several centuries, is being edged out of its central role. The moderate brand of Islam will not be reinstated in its former position unless the factors making up the equation of internal collapse, to which Islamic societies are exposed, are solved.

A third factor has been the international situation. Unless the outside world realizes that adopting a hostile position towards Islam and Muslims indiscriminately can only provoke negative reactions, the moderate brand will not be reinstated. This is all the more true given that they were partners with those responsible for starting the downward spiral and helped bring about the series of external factors that allowed the cycle of violence to attain its present level.

Humanity's failure to support and reinforce the gentle, non-militant brand of Islam, to which most Islamic societies until recently belonged, by helping remove the internal and external 'landmines' which eroded the ability of those societies to stand up to the assault of militant Islam is a crime committed by humanity against itself; it is a crime for which it will pay an exorbitant price. Thus the question regarding the future of the Muslim mind remains the same as the question over the future of Islamic societies: is it a future of freedom, democracy, prosperity and progress, or the opposite? The answer to this question will determine the answer to the question about the future of the Muslim mind: will it follow the route of moderate Islam or that of Wahhabi Islam?

Speeding up political, economic and educational reform is the only way to reduce the illogical popularity of Islamism. Once people in

Muslim societies start to reap the benefits of freedom and active participation, coupled with a marked improvement in their economic and living conditions together with real educational reform, their admiration for Islamist groups will wane, and they will realize that their welfare will not come at the hands of groups whose leaders are fanatical, narrow-minded and out of touch with the requirements of the age.

Despair, deplorable living conditions, feelings of injustice, the harsh realities of life and rampant corruption constitute the ideal environment for converts to the ideology of political Islam, which offers 'hope' in an atmosphere of hopelessness. But offering hope is one thing, while making good on the offer, quite a different matter. The Islamists are selling dreams, mirages and false promises professing that they have a formula to cure all of society's ills. In reality, however, they lack the competence required to undertake such a task. Progress is a modern management concept that can be achieved by anyone – Christians, Jews, Muslims and Buddhists – as long as its elements are available. These elements are political, managerial, economic, educational, and humanistic, regardless of religion or nationality.

THE WEAPONS OF TERRORISM

A. Advocates or Followers?

The word terrorism has been used to describe the activities of various groups over the last half century. For example, the British denounced the operations carried out by the Irish Republican Army as terrorism, while the same description was applied to the activities of such militant groups as the Basque revolutionary group Euskadi Ta Askatasuna (ETA, Fatherland and Liberty), the organization seeking autonomy for the Basque region lying between Spain and France; the Red Brigades in Italy; the Baader-Meinhof Gang in Germany; the Red Army in Japan, and similar movements in Latin America.

However, when the word terrorism is mentioned today, what immediately springs to mind (in societies other than the Arab and Muslim) is that an Arab or Muslim has committed an act of violence. The linkage between terrorism and Muslims has grown over the last six years, giving rise to the irrational fear of Islam known as 'Islamophobia'. In fact there is no doubt that Muslims or Arabs are usually implicated in acts that are today described by the world as terrorism. When it comes to addressing this phenomenon, there are two main schools of thought: one condemns Muslims in absolute terms, the other (Islamic) school justifies it as a reaction to the circumstances in which Muslims have found themselves.

A novel approach used here is to identify the sources or pillars of a phenomenon that has become one of the main areas of concern throughout the world. The Arab/Muslim model of terrorism differs from others in terms of magnitude due to the greater number of followers it can claim. In other words, while the advocates of this form of terrorism are few in number and comparable to those operating in other cultural and religious contexts, the number of disciples attracted to the ideas propounded by the advocates of violence in the Islamic case is considerably larger.

There is a crucial distinction between 'advocates' and 'followers', which is the key to finding solutions and dealing successfully with a phenomenon seen by many outside the Muslim communities as the greatest challenge to humankind and civilization in the twenty-first century. Advocates who try to win over adherents to their cause cannot attract large numbers of followers unless the mental and psychological state of their audience and the political, economic and social conditions in which their prospective followers live make them receptive to the message. In all religions, sects and ethnicities there are advocates who disseminate extremely radical and sometimes extremely aggressive ideas. But the number of followers who adopt those ideas differs from one case to another.

For example, some Jewish and Christian leaders advocate ideas totally at odds with common humanity, with tolerance and acceptance of the 'Other'. Indeed, they sometimes call for death to others. But the number of followers who espouse their cause is nowhere close to the number of those whom advocates of some extremist Islamic ideas succeed in winning over. Many political regimes (unfortunately supported by some members of the intelligentsia) lump the members of both groups – advocates and followers – together and deal with them through the state's security apparatus – an approach that only compounds the problem. Although the advocates of violence through words are dangerous, the security risk they represent is limited. Their message cannot in and of itself push any society to the point reached by a number of Muslim societies today. Using police methods against them will not produce positive results. Indeed, it could be counterproductive.

Take the case of Sayyid Qutb, the Islamist thinker executed by the Egyptian government in 1966. His ideas survived his death to become, after their merger with the Wahhabi doctrine, the primary ideological source on which most of the radical movements of political Islam draw today. The only way to curtail the influence wielded by the advocates of violence is through a concerted cultural and ideological campaign by enlightened members of the intelligentsia. For ideas can only be fought with ideas, beliefs with beliefs. And if the campaign is to succeed it will not be thanks to 'official' intellectuals who lack any credibility and who are more bureaucrats than independent thinkers.

In the final analysis, however, it is not the advocates of violence but their followers who constitute the cornerstone of the phenomenon known as Islamic terrorism. The solution to the problem of political violence justified in the name of Islam lies in the answer to the following question: What draws people in many Muslim societies, particularly the young, into the web of advocates who teach radical ideas, justify violence, and call on them to isolate themselves from the course of human civilization?

The answer to the appeal that advocates of violence have for the young in Muslim societies can be summed up in one word: 'anger'. The sources of this anger are many, and rather than condemning it, efforts should be made to understand it. If understanding leads to compassion, there is nothing wrong with that. From a humanistic and historical perspective, to understand and sympathize is not to condone, justify or accept. Rather, it is to recognize that we are dealing with patients suffering from a debilitating and dangerous disease; patients who need treatment, not security procedures, violence, coercion and torture.

B. The Pillars beneath Proliferation

The main – but not the only – sources of anger among young people in many Muslim societies include:

- The well-founded fear that their prospects for making a decent living are extremely limited. Whether educated or uneducated, they are unable to find suitable employment that can provide them with a reasonable standard of living.
- The enormous gap between the haves and have-nots; not so much the fact that there is a gap, as its sheer magnitude.
- The ambiguity surrounding how the wealthy acquire their

fortunes, the powerful their power, and the famous their fame. This was not always the case. For example, people knew that Muhammad Tala'at Harb,[1] the Egyptian economist and banker of the 1920s era, was a rich man, but they never thought he had amassed his wealth through dubious means.

- The disappearance of fairness from most fields of employment and occasionally even from commercial activities, where cronyism counts for more than merit, and where those who enjoy the backing of political muscle (which is not available to the vast majority) are assured of success and advancement.
- The absence of personalities with leadership qualities in most areas.
- The close relationship that exists between the plutocrats, the executive branch of government and the media.
- Rumours about corruption in high places that, despite the absence of concrete evidence, people tend to believe.

A study of these seven pillars on which the anger which spawns violence, rejection, hostility and terrorism rests is a political, cultural and strategic matter. To address them exclusively from a security perspective does a grave injustice to society and to all the parties concerned, including the security institutions themselves. In the long run, police methods are no solution to phenomena with numerous political, economic, social and cultural dimensions.

NOTE

1. 1867–1941. Egyptian economist, co-founder of *Banque Misr* in 1920.

3

The Illusion of 'Religious' Parties

I. HUMAN DISTORTION

There is more than one logical and sound reason to refuse the establishment of political parties based solely on religious platforms. First, glorification and sanctification of Islamic *fiqh* (jurisprudence) is a baseless act because it is merely a man-made interpretation of holy texts according to the most fixed and widespread definition of Islamic *fiqh*: '*Fiqh* is the science concerned with the deduction of practical rules out of their juristic references', a process of deduction that is a human, not a divine action as it inevitably requires the use of language and logic.

A further proof of the temporal nature of *fiqh* is the legacy of the great Sunni jurists – Abu Hanifa, Malik, al-Shafi'i, and Ahmad Ibn Hanbal – who created this jurisprudence in less than two hundred years. In addition, Malik and al-Shafi'i, although contemporaries, differed in their opinions regarding *fiqh*. Malik also published a jurisprudential *madhhab* (school or legal system) different from that of Abu Hanifa, and al-Shafi'i produced two different legal systems, one for Iraq and another for Egypt.[1]

Consequently, the principles considered by some to be the Islamic tenets for comprehensive systems of government are nothing but *ijtihad*.[2] Such interpretations have come to be called the 'Sultanic' commandments. Experts know that temporal rulers, whether during the Umayyad or the Abbasid eras, heavily influenced most of what was written about the Sultanic commandments. These rulers acted this way in order to guarantee that whatever was written about the laws would concur with their desires and understanding concerning the governance of their respective communities. Of course, similar processes occurred in other places.

Thus, the existence of political parties formed on a religious basis alone is illogical because the principles of the so-called Islamic doctrine in government affairs are entirely a human production. They reflect nothing but the interpretations of humans, who could be right or wrong. Islam does not articulate a comprehensive framework for organizing government systems that could replace the contemporary details found within a constitution. Outlining such detailed schemes was neither the task nor the aim of Islam. However, blaming Islam for not presenting a distinct political system is tantamount to blaming it for not having a comprehensive theory in psychology, sociology or management sciences. In fact, Islam came with a whole host of general rules which would be more useful as guidelines when formulating the more detailed constitutional arrangments. Taking al-Mawardi's[3] eleventh-century *The Sultanic Commandments* (*al-Ahkam al-Sultaniyya*), which later became a genre of its own with many volumes devoted to the same topic, as examples for such detailed regulations is preferable to demanding too much from vague Islamic statements. Those works are man-made *ijtihad*, which reflect the authors' academic and rational abilities, as well as their cultural and motivational backgrounds, while also bearing in mind the unavoidable impact of historical and geographical factors.

Thus there is a clear and powerful logic that can eradicate the viewpoint calling for the establishment of political parties based on religious platforms. What some call 'systems of governorship in Islam' were merely the deductions of men who lived more than one thousand years ago and established the rules that they thought – in their time and place and within the terms of their understanding, knowledge and conditions – would lead to the foundation of a governing system representing the essential values of Islam. Thus, the so-called 'ruling system in Islam' is a vague and imprecise description of what Muslim jurists wrote more than one thousand years ago in a serious and respected attempt to form polities that would govern their communities in harmony with the principles and values of Islam.

II. TEMPORAL DILEMMA

The writings of ancient Muslim scholars with regard to laws and government are valuable attempts that have been inspired by the essence of Islam. If that hypothesis is accepted, then there has been a lack of ambition within the Muslim community for over one thousand years to update and expand these political traditions, and it is necessary to revise the writings of the ancient jurists regarding the

Sultanic commandments in order to reform contemporary political and constitutional regulations.

Thus any discussion supported by writings published a millennium ago and ignoring contemporary Islamic jurisprudential issues will be just like using a book compiled in the tenth century AD on medicine and pharmacology as a touchstone to establish modern medical systems and institutions. Such a course of action would inevitably lead to the death of all the patients.

Islam spoke about donkeys and cattle as important means of transportation. It also spoke about the principle of *shura* (consultation), but not directly about democracy, citizenship and human rights. Nevertheless, it is shameful for a modern man to insist on using donkeys as his only means of transportation. This kind of decision led to the conflict between Wahhabis, headed by Faysal al-Da'waysh, and King Abd al-Aziz,[4] when the Wahhabis rejected all the conveniences of modern civilization such as cars, telephones and radios.[5] The individual who insists on solely using the concept of *shura* is like the person who believes that means of transportation should be restricted to donkeys and cattle, on the grounds that Islam spoke about donkeys and did not speak about cars, trains or planes. Current political realities beg the question, 'Why can't we, as Muslims, establish political parties based on religious platforms?' There are numerous political parties in Europe described as 'Christian', the most well-known of them being probably the German Christian Democratic Party. And yet in the constitutions of all countries which have Christian parties and in those parties' platforms there is not a single word that implies those parties will rule according to religious fundamentals but rather according to the values contained in their respective constitutions. These parties are Christian in name only; they are political parties representing conservative viewpoints of a secular nature. Although their principles and values have been inspired by Christianity, they rule and are ruled by the terms of their constitutions and positive laws. Supporters of a movement such as the Muslim Brotherhood in Egypt would never dare to announce that their goal in transferring the Brotherhood into a political party is to reach a similar frame of mind as that of the Christian democratic parties in Europe.

There remains one important argument. Political parties which describe themselves as Islamic are acting purely as political bodies. They are simply political entities seeking power. In and of themselves, these goals are legal objectives. Yet some of these parties play on emotional chords when they describe themselves as Islamic. They are nothing but a *salafi* (fundamentalist) movement living off the understandings and deductions of individuals who lived more than ten centuries ago and handled the issues of their age through solutions that were consequences of their time and place. There is no better evidence than that Muhammad Ibn Idris (Imam al-Shafi'i) published a new legal system when he arrived in Egypt, as his previously published legal doctrine was suitable only for a distinct body politic in Iraq.

It is catastrophic when a people refuses to update a political doctrine for one thousand years and wants to continue to be ruled on the understandings of others who worked hard and made every effort ten centuries ago to establish polities for their era. Islam touched on lofty values concerning justice, equality and the virtues of knowledge. Nevertheless, Islam, in order to be suitable for times and places other than during its dawning, did not articulate detailed specific codes. As such, followers of political Islamic streams of thought are fighting to establish a comprehensive governing system that is not applicable in the modern era. Islam has not prescribed such a detailed system. Therefore, political Islamic movements end up clinging to themes that have little relevance in the modern era, such as the impermissibility of bank interests in Islam[6] and the penal code, among others.[7]

The best option for Islamic political movements would be to admit that Islam is a sublime religion and not a book about economics, politics, sociology, psychology, chemistry or medicine. However, if they make this admission, how will they play the game of politics? If they make it, they will abandon the strongest tool of their political propaganda. In addition, they will be required to present a realistic political, economic and social programme and not their usual tricks and slogans of 'applying God's commands', 'Islam is the solution' and '*al-baraka*' (the blessing). Such abstract and commonplace slogans, if examined in the practical battlefield of life, would prove to be nothing but big empty air bubbles that contain mere politics and no religion whatsoever.

III. IN SEARCH OF 'BLESSINGS'

Regarding the issue of the 'blessing', many kind, simple Muslims think that having people ruling in the name of Islam at the helm of the community is enough to bring welfare and blessing. To those who think this way, note that early Muslims – including the Prophet himself – were defeated in the battle of Uhud (625 AD). If victory, success, progress or welfare were achievable through blessings alone, Muslims would have been victorious at Uhud, as they clearly had the blessing of the Prophet. However, the defeat of Muslims at Uhud proves that just as God created all creatures of the world, he also created certain rules and laws to run the universe, amongst them the laws of nature.

One of these laws says that whoever fights without the material and practical qualifications of victory will be defeated. Through these laws Muslims, led by Tariq Ibn Ziyyad[8] in the ninth century, won in their conquest of Andalusia and, because of the very same laws, Muslims were defeated in 732 at the Battle of Tours in southern France.[9]

Whoever thinks that blessings will come upon him just because he says that he is ruling in the name of Islam will receive results in all fields similar to the defeat in the Battle of Uhud. Victory, progress and successful leadership come only through science and good administration, which are human tenets that are universal and belong to no religion, denomination or nationality. There is no evidence that those who want to rule their communities in the name of religion acquire any such tenets. On the contrary, we have evidence acquired from their backgrounds, ideological history and relationship with the universality of science, knowledge and the values of progress that they do not and will never acquire these tenets.

IV 'PIETY' UNVEILED

Many in Egypt today are talking about two features that have come to dominate the country's social landscape. The first is that manifestations of piety have become far more widespread in recent times than they were a century ago. The second is that there is a noticeable upsurge in behavioural aberrations at the societal level, where tension, violence, aggression and lack of civility in dealings between members of society have become the norm.

While neither of these observations can be denied, there is a contradiction between them. If the religiosity that has come to permeate society's cultural climate, and the manifestations of piety displayed by its members, have not prevented the decline in moral standards, civility and social ethics, this can only mean that piety, or, more accurately, the understanding of piety that has come to prevail, does not serve the interests of society. This is by no means to deny that there are among those who subscribe to this understanding of piety admirable examples of moral rectitude.

This contradiction can only be resolved if it is noted that what has come to be called piety is in fact not piety at all. Egypt is swamped by such ostentatious displays of piety as women wrapped in what has come to be called 'Islamic' dress and men sporting beards, wearing silver – as opposed to gold – wedding bands, and bearing marks on their foreheads attesting to the hours they spent prostrating themselves on prayer rugs. Not to mention how the senses are constantly assailed – in writing, from the pulpit, and through the media – by voices urging the faithful to observe the ritualistic aspects of religion. If some are entitled to consider that this constitutes piety then, by the same token, others, including the writer of these lines, are entitled to assert that rites and rituals have absolutely nothing to do with real piety.

To be pious is to live by a strong moral code, to be helpful to others, and to display such noble character traits as altruism, tolerance and a strong work ethic. As to the manifestations of piety mentioned, they are due to a combination of political, economic, social, educational, cultural and psychological factors that can be easily identified. According to the Positivist school of philosophy founded by the nineteenth-century French thinker, Auguste Comte, no one can claim that greater religiosity will set things right, because practical experience proves that excessive religiosity could further promote the decline in general standards of behaviour, as well as the violence and anger in dealings among people.[10]

The ubiquitous religiosity witnessed today in the form of a rigid adherence to the ritualistic aspects of religious observance stems from a variety of sources:

- More than half a century of no political participation or fictitious political participation.
- More than half a century of economic decline and the erosion of the middle class.
- The complete divorce between the Egyptian educational system and what is happening in the rest of the world, its isolation from

modern systems of education and its reflection of cultural defects such as the growing tendency toward insularity, bigotry and the lack of critical thinking.
- The succession of oligarchies that have governed political and social life for over half a century is also a source of the excessive religiosity to which society has succumbed.

Added to all of the above is the deteriorating quality and standard of the religious establishment, which has been infected by ideas from the east. Further, there is the absence from the scene of anything other than religion that can nurture a sense of belonging among Egypt's youth. Immersing themselves in the rituals of religious observance has become a psychological refuge for those who find nothing else to which they can anchor themselves in a time of uncertainty, for want of any hope, a class, an ambition, a party, a better reality, or a specific cultural model.

Every person on the face of the earth (with the exception of a small minority whose only allegiance is to their own ideas, principles and value systems) needs to feel that he or she 'belongs' to something or other. In advanced societies whose members enjoy a high standard of living, people's sense of belonging can take a variety of forms. There are those whose allegiance is to their own personal successes, others to a political party, to a certain social class with its own culture and value system, or to a specific ideological or cultural movement. Through this feeling of belonging, a person achieves the satisfaction and fulfilment necessary for the well-being of every individual. This can help explain the sense of belonging which Egyptians felt for the national movement led by Saad Zaghlul[11] in the 1920s, as well as why most of the Egyptian people identified so closely with the Nasserite project a few decades later. In both cases, there was a movement that succeeded in gaining the allegiance of broad segments of society, irrespective of how successful either was in making good on its promises or living up to its slogans.

With the disappearance of these movements, which attracted the interest, energies, loyalty and allegiance of most members of society, the field was left wide open for a different kind of allegiance to take hold, one that is more appealing, comfortable, and, because given to generalities and lack of precision, suitable for men and women of an average cultural formation. Where allegiance to Marxism, for example, requires an above-average degree of awareness, culture and intelligence, this does not apply when it comes to simply subscribing to religious slogans. Religious slogans – which are in fact purely political and not religious at all – owe their appeal to the regression and erosion of the roles played by other movements which were highly effective at earlier stages of our modern history over the last two centuries.

Ritualistic piety (as endorsed in the writings of men like Ibn Taymiyya and Ibn Qayyim al-Jawziyya and in the applications of Muhammad Ibn Abd al-Wahhab and the experiences inspired by his school) works on the outer, not the inner, person. It is like a particularly strict traffic system that lays down rigorous rules determining what people can and cannot do. It is a school of thinking that may be suitable for primitive communities with a limited store of education, culture and knowledge but not for contemporary, advanced and civilized societies. Communities governed by this strict code could appear to be disciplined on the outside but are riddled with defects and shortcomings. It treats people like circus animals trained with whips to follow the routine laid down for them. But piety, in the sense by which it is understood in Sufism, Christianity, and Buddhism, works on the inner person and seeks to have what is good in human nature triumph over its aggressive and base aspects.

It is no coincidence that Islamic societies governed by the strictest religious rules, that is, rules designed to maintain an outer semblance of piety, are the most dissolute, the most unhealthily obsessed with sexuality and all forms of sensual indulgence. The attempt to control these aberrations on the 'outside' without trying to deal with the 'inside' creates a kind of dichotomy, a pathological split between what is said in public and what is done in private that is perhaps without parallel in the world.

NOTES

1. Mohamed ibn Idris Al-Shafii, *Al'um* [Mother], rev. edn (Beirut: Dar Al-Kotob Al-Ilmiyah, 2009).
2. Independent interpretation of the legal sources in Islam.
3. 972–1058. Muslim jurist from the Abbasid era.
4. 1880–1953. First king of Saudi Arabia.
5. Laurence W. Thomas, *Three Autobiographies: The Autobiography Of Larry W. Larry, Flights From Arabia, The Anderson File*, (Authorhouse, 2002).
6. http://www.islamonline.net/servlet/Satellite?pagename=IslamOnline-English-Ask_Scholar/FatwaE/FatwaE&cid=1119503543118.
7. http://www.renaissance.com.pk/septfeart2y2.html.
8. Eighth century AD. Berber Umayyad Muslim leader, one of the most important military commanders in Iberia.
9. Also known as the Battle of Poitiers, 732 AD.
10. See Harriet Martineau, *The Positive Philosophy of Auguste Comte*, available at: http://socserv.mcmaster.ca/econ/ugcm/3ll3/comte/Philosophy1.pdf.
11. 1859–1927. Egyptian political figure; served as prime minister of Egypt from 26 January 1924 to 24 November 1924.

4

Vision … or Nightmare?

- Mahmud Fahmi al-Nuqrashi, Gamal Abdel Nasser, Anwar Sadat and Hosni Mubarak were the chief executives of Egypt throughout most of the last sixty years of the twentieth century. All were targeted for assassination by Islamist groups who succeeded in gunning down two of their intended victims, Nuqrashi and Sadat.
- In the misguided belief that they could contain one of the most important leaders of those groups in Egypt, the Americans granted Umar Abd al-Rahman, leader of the Egyptian terrorist Islamic Group (al-Gama'at al-Islamiyya) an entry visa to the United States. No sooner had he settled down, however, than he orchestrated the first attack on the World Trade Centre. He is now serving life in prison.

These are only two of the depressing examples of facts that come to mind when people talk of the need to include Islamists in Egypt's political life. The prospect of giving these throwbacks to the Dark Ages a say in how Egyptians should run their lives is daunting when one thinks of their attitude toward women or Copts, groups to which they accord a status only slightly higher than that of prisoners of war or slaves.

To imagine a scenario in which the 'Islamists' will have achieved all their objectives and proceed to impose their vision of what the Muslim world should be would include such principal features as:

- The departure of the West, particularly the United States, from Muslim lands.
- The removal of the kings and presidents now in power for being what bin Laden and his ilk see as agents of the United States.
- The takeover of power by Osama bin Laden or someone like him, the reinstatement of the Caliphate, the annulment of existing law, and the adoption of their version of Islamic Sharia.

Where would this lead? Such a scenario could unfold in two ways.

One would be the complete isolation of the Muslim world from the non-Muslim world in all spheres: scientific, economic, military and cultural. Islamic societies would be transformed into vast seas of humanity with little knowledge of science or of how its application can improve the quality of life on earth. Of course, this matters little to a Muslim who is more concerned with what happens to him in the afterlife than he is with his lot in this life, which to him is but an instant in the greater scheme of things, a passage to the hereafter. Under political Islam these societies will be densely populated because their rulers will tell them that the Sharia enjoins Muslims to multiply, as this will make the Prophet proud of them on Judgment Day. The living standard of the members of these societies, which will have boycotted sacrilegious Western science, will be dismal in all respects. But this, too, is unimportant, because the material world is of little significance to the devout fundamentalist Muslim, who considers life to be but a short bridge he must traverse to reach either Heaven (with its flowing streams, succulent fruits and black-eyed virgins), or Hell (with its raging fires).

Such a society would encourage raids on the world of the infidels, with the infidels retaliating in kind, their advanced weapons raining widespread devastation on the Muslim world and turning it into an empty wasteland where backwardness and chaos reign supreme. For the Muslims, who do not manufacture their own weapons but are forced to buy them from their more advanced enemies, have no way of defending themselves against the sophisticated weapons used against them.

One can practically hear the imams in the mosques assuring their congregations that God inflicted the defeat on them to test their faith, and that if they pass the test He would send them a miraculous victory. Thundering from their pulpits (*minbars*) they will paint a rosy picture of the Muslims triumphing over the unbelievers, ending their sermon by calling on God to wreak death and destruction on the pagan Christians and their Jewish lackeys.

The second way in which the scenario could unfold assumes that the leaders of political Islam, after achieving the objectives mentioned above, will not set out to isolate the Muslim from the non-Muslim world. Instead, they will deal with the unbelievers in accordance with an established maxim of Islamic jurisprudence which holds that 'necessity overrides taboos'. In this scenario, there will be extensive transactions with the non-Muslim world in all sectors: economic, scientific, social, industrial, agricultural and services. The acquisition of knowledge will be a high priority goal on the grounds that Muslims 'must seek knowledge, even in China'.

Yet this less frightening scenario would inevitably take Muslim communities back to where they stood a century ago when it came to dealing with non-Muslims: one party learning from the other, one party buying from the other, one party trying to catch up with the other.

But whether the first scenario prevails or the second, the big question remains the same: why the suffering, the spilt blood, the violence and destruction, the pain, anxiety and misery? In these two scenarios, power will lie with the 'Islamists'. In a scenario where things remain as they are, the outcome is equally dismal.

There is, however, a third scenario which assumes that Muslim societies will opt for development, progress and democracy, in which case power will lie with the people who will exercise it through their duly elected representatives. Unfortunately, this last scenario is not receiving serious consideration in political circles.

I. THE USE OF FORCE

A. Deployment of Muscles

Many of the storms engulfing our part of the world can be attributed to the fact that the movements practising politics in the name of 'political Islam' are still governed by a coup mentality, still acting as underground movements rather than as modern political institutions that respect and observe the law. Actually, the word 'mentality', which assumes the use of mental faculties, is a misnomer in this case, as most of these movements rely more on their muscles than their brains, more on raw power than on minds governed by a respect for laws, constitutions, rationality and sound judgment.

1. Unfortunate Events

Take the case of Lebanon, which has an elected government and a parliament representing the people; and yet the largest opposition movement, a religio-political organization, refuses to recognize the authority of the nation's elected representatives and listens only to strident voices calling for a return to the past. The religious firebrands seeking to drive Lebanon centuries back in time are playing a game in which the muscles of blind power ride roughshod over the principles of democracy, constitutional legitimacy and the rule of law. A single armed party, Hezbollah, is turning the tables on everyone, and showing total contempt for the elected parliament that should be the ultimate arbiter, instead of hordes of demonstrators manipulated from outside the country by a theocratic regime that is financing the destruction of Lebanon.

Then there is the situation in the Palestinian self-ruled territories, where a theocratic movement, Hamas, emerging from the cobwebs of medieval times, does not consider itself bound by any of the commitments undertaken by previous governments. As far as it is concerned, events only began to unfold the day it came to power. When Abu Mazen, leader of the Palestinian Authority, wisely, if somewhat belatedly, called for a return to the people, the source of authority, the government of theocrats whose understanding of democracy is limited to its usefulness as a means of reaching power, rejected his call.

A theocratic movement that is by definition democratically immature may be capable of understanding that democracy brought it to power but not that it will, by the same token, prevent it from hanging on to power indefinitely. Governed as they are by a coup mentality totally at odds with the very notion of democracy, the members of this movement are driven by religious hysteria (not religious faith), coupled with a violent and confrontational style of political action.

The movements of political Islam have not yet gone through the necessary stage of threshing out their ideas – of separating the chaff from the grain, so to speak. Nor have these movements seen any internal ideological developments to speak of. Indeed, Muslim thinking was exposed to many more radical changes in the hundred years separating the death of the first of the four great Sunni jurists – Abu Hanifa al-Nu'man (in the middle of the second century of the Hijra calendar), and the death of the last – Ahmad Ibn Hanbal (just over a century later) – than in the twelve centuries since Ibn Hanbal's death in the third century of the Hijra calendar.

2. Coincidence or a Mentality?

It is interesting to speculate on the similarity between what

Hezbollah did in Lebanon in May 2008 – when its militia took over Beirut to force the government to back down on several decrees, with the death of 100 Lebanese – and what Hamas did in Gaza in June 2007 when it seized control of the Gaza Strip, killing about 100 Palestinians. The fact that both displayed the same pattern of behaviour shows the mentality shared by all Islamic fundamentalists, Sunni and Shia alike.

Theocrats, whose political beliefs are a function of their religious convictions, may claim to believe in democracy, modern state systems, pluralism and diversity (that is, the acceptance of and respect for the rights of the 'Other'), but do so purely for reasons of expediency. They know full well that paying lip service to such noble sentiments – if only at a certain stage – can serve their interests and avert problems.

In fact, a fundamentalist who practises politics is driven by the conviction that God is on his side and that he is the conduit through which the Almighty's will is transmitted to the world of politics. There is thus no room in a fundamentalist's system of beliefs for such notions as democracy, rotation of power, pluralism or diversity. In Iran, for example, it is the supreme guide who not only lays down higher state policies but also enters into such minutiae of the country's political life as deciding whether or not a candidate is entitled to run for parliamentary elections. Then there is the case of Palestinian political life, where brazen disregard for democracy was displayed by the Hamas leadership. Although it was democracy that brought them to power, no sooner were they installed in the seat of authority than they set out to trample it underfoot. Transformed into an instrument of tyranny and repression, the Hamas government began to eliminate its opponents systematically, not symbolically but physically. In some cases, they were executed in a particularly brutal fashion, such as being thrown off high buildings. It should be no surprise that those who mix religion with politics should resort to such barbaric practices. Political religion – not religion itself – is an example of a closed system where any deviation from the official line, deemed as the only true path, is not tolerated.

What Hezbollah did in Lebanon is a new version of the diabolical game that mixes politics with religion. Not content with taking Lebanon to war in 2006 without the consent of the state, a war from which it claimed to have emerged victorious thanks to divine intervention (a victory that exists only in the imagination of some deluded souls) Hezbollah, which is a state within a state, more accurately, a state *outside* the state, installed a private cable communication network. After the government issued a decree outlawing the network, Hezbollah militias swept through Beirut and, in an act that epitomizes the way their mind works, set fire to the building housing the Mustaqbal television channel, owned by the leader of the rival and governing party.

The similarity between the actions of Iran's Supreme Guide Ali Khomeini in deciding who can run for office; of Hamas in Gaza, from throwing their opponents off high buildings to instigating incursions across Egypt's borders; and of Hezbollah in occupying Beirut to impose its will on political opponents is no coincidence. All these actions attest to the medieval mentality of their protagonists, a mentality that is inimical to freedom, democracy and modern state systems. The world will pay a heavy price if it stands passively by while this drags entire societies back to the first millennium as humanity moves into the third millennium.

II. 'DIVINE DOMINION'

Many hurdles stand between the trends espousing political Islam, including the Muslim Brotherhood, and political maturity. Perhaps the most insurmountable is their clinging to the theory of *hakamiyya* or 'divine dominion' propounded by Abu Ala al-Mawdudi, the Pakistani theorist of radical Islamism who died in 1979, and Sayyid Qutb. Derived from the Arabic root '*hukm*', which means rule, the theory has a certain superficial glitter that appeals to some people. In fact, however, it is based on an untenable proposition that renders it meaningless.

The theory of *hakamiyya* postulates that mortals are not ruled by mortals but by God. This is dangerous sophistry, as there is no direct recourse to the Supreme Being, in the literal sense of the word 'direct', given the existence of a religious caste ruling in His name, and according to their own strict understanding of His intentions. The two thinkers came up with their theory, a fanciful notion that can obviously not be implemented in practice, each in reaction to his own personal traumatic experience. Both men experienced what we now call a culture shock, Mawdudi in the face of the strong and vibrant culture of India, Qutb, who spent less than two years in the United States in the early 1950s, in the face of an American culture that shocked him to the core. Unable to cope with the realities of the age, they chose to escape into a less challenging past.

Thus the first obstacle that the movements of political Islam must overcome if they want to live in the modern age at peace with the rest of humanity is the theory of *hakamiyya*, to which all adherents of these movements subscribe. For it is a theory which cannot be applied unless we turn the clock back more than a thousand years and regard all other cultures as mortal enemies.

III. DEMOCRACY, THE SALVATION

The next step is for the leaders of these movements to develop a better understanding of, and a stronger faith in, democracy among their followers. They need to explain democracy as a process distinct from *shura* (consultation). Although there is no contradiction between them, *shura* is but one part of a whole, namely, democracy. To those who consider this as belittling Islam, I would like to point out that while it is true that Islam spoke of *shura* and not of democracy, it is also true that it spoke of pack animals and not of cars and planes. This in no way detracts from the greatness of Islam. After all, the purpose of Islam's message was not to predict the achievements of future ages, such as democracy, planes, human rights, lasers, medical breakthroughs, civil management systems, information technology, etc.

The leaders of political Islam movements need to breed a new generation of followers who believe that the nation is the source of authority, that the constitution is the law of laws, and that in this day and age societies cannot be led by men of religion (especially when the religion in question does not allow a caste of clerics to act as intermediaries between man and God), but by the latest discoveries in science, management, ideas and information technology.

Until at least some of these leaders break away from the doctrinaire approach to religion that has plagued the Muslim mind for over a thousand years, and unless they can groom generations capable of understanding that the nation is the source of all power and that societies can only be run by science and management, we should not be surprised to find the young members of Islamist movements trying to form militias in a bid to govern us with wild emotions, strident voices, and muscle power untamed by reason or common sense.

These were the main features of the prevailing storm of intolerant

Islam. But did such a storm reach that powerful condition, outreach and influence without a strong and rich breeder and custodian? The answer is 'certainly not'. Did it find a suitable patronage? It certainly did. The storm that currently threatens the cornerstones of humanity, progress and modernity was well patronized; and this was by a patron that has been sitting on more than a quarter of the remaining oil reserves of the entire world.

5

The Breeder

I. THE KING AND THE SWORD

In November 2007 there occurred a symbolically disturbing act when the king of Saudi Arabia presented the Pope with a sword during his visit to the Vatican. It came at a time when there has never been a greater need to distance the name of Islam and the image of Muslims from the violent connotations and symbolism of the sword. The Saudi monarch's unfortunate choice of a gift prompted me to write the address he might better have delivered if his advisors had been familiar with the Western culture and mindset.

> Your Holiness … Your Eminences … in the name of Saudi Arabia that I am honoured to represent, and in the name of Islam to which I am honoured to belong, I bring you greetings of peace. In fact, the word 'Islam' in Arabic is an anagram of the word 'peace'. On my behalf, and on behalf of the people I represent, I say let us embark on a new era based on mutual respect; an era in which neither party hurts the feelings of the other, and both refrain from aggression, moral or material, direct or indirect, against one another. I call on you and on the belief I represent to pledge that the followers of any religion, while entitled to invite others into their faith, may not resort to violence, coercion or the use of swords, but to resort instead to persuasion and reasoning to convince them of the merits of the faith to which they belong. I hereby declare that from this day forth, '*jihad*' means only self-defence and resistance to aggression, but never the initiation of conflict, or the attempt to convert others to our religion by means of violence or the sword. There is nothing more pathetic than a religion that cannot win the hearts and minds of people except through the use of the sword. I also urge all parties to be more concerned with the quality of the followers of each religion than with their quantity. In this connection, there is much to be done to improve the quality of the believers of our great religion.

I call on you and on the belief I represent to refrain from mocking or insulting the 'Other', and belittling their beliefs or disparaging their sacred texts. I call on you and on the belief I represent to usher in a new era in which all shall enjoy freedom of belief, freedom of worship, and the freedom to build houses of worship in any place at any time. As the Prophet of Islam welcomed the Christians of Najran [in the south-western Arabian Peninsula] when they came, allowing them to pray in his mosque, which is now known as the Prophet's Mosque in the holy city of Medina, I declare before you that we shall begin a new chapter of dealing with non-Muslims as our brothers in humanity. I shall call on all Muslims in the world to consider such terms as *Dar al-Harb* (Land of War), *Dar al-Salam* (Land of Peace) and *Ahl al-Dhimma* (non-Muslim monotheists) to be products of historical conditions of a bygone age that are no longer applicable today, and that we now aspire to a world that is not divided into camps of war and camps of peace. Our mosques shall welcome all who step through their doors, and our religion is a confident religion that does not force anyone to remain a prisoner of its precepts.

Your Holiness, I have chosen two gifts to present to you today. One is a golden palm tree that symbolizes our history and environment, the other an ancient manuscript of the Bible dating back many centuries. I turned down a proposal to present you with a sword, because first, the sword is not one of your historical symbols, and second, we do not want the message it carries to cloud our future relationship. My country will make every effort to ensure that, in future, foreigners in our land be made to feel welcome, that they enjoy warm hospitality and tolerance in every sense of the word, including the right to pray and worship God in churches or temples according to their faith. The sight of churches' spires or temples' domes rising against our skyline will not hurt our feelings, exactly as seeing the minarets of mosques in Europe, America, Canada and Australia does not hurt the feelings of non-Muslims in those places.

I also vow before you that we shall very shortly look into not applying laws derived from our religion to the followers of other faiths. Let us begin a new era of accepting the other, of tolerance and of fostering the concept of 'relativism' in the area of religious beliefs, that is, let no person on the face of the earth behave as though his/her religion is the absolute truth, while all other religions are absolutely false. Let God decide matters we are neither required nor equipped to concern ourselves with. I call on you and on all those I represent to enter a new era of tolerance, acceptance of the other and mutual respect, in which all desist from demeaning the faiths of others.

I would like to take the opportunity of this meeting to propose the formation of a committee made up of the best religious scholars from all faiths, not only of the three great Abrahamic or religions of the Book, but of all other faiths as well, to review educational curricula throughout the world, in order to achieve the following aims:

- Remove from the curricula any material offensive or prejudicial to the faith of others.
- Remove from the curricula any material that sows the seeds of religious chauvinism and feelings of superiority over other faiths.
- Remove from the curricula any material that discourages tolerance and acceptance of the other and replace it with material that promotes admiration for diversity and variety as the most important features of life and the main sources of its richness and beauty.

Let me now present Your Holiness with the golden palm tree and the manuscript of the Bible that dates back to the spread of Christianity in the region of Najran, today one of the governorates making up the Kingdom of Saudi Arabia.

This, then, is the speech the king did not make, and which could have helped usher in a new era of empathy and understanding between peoples of all faiths.

II. THE INOCULATION OF HATRED

The sociology of the tribes of the Arabian Peninsula is the key to understanding the Arab fundamentalist mentality, and the lack of tolerance for the 'Other'. In order to trace the historical features of that character, mentality and intolerance we must try to imagine the way of life in the inland wastes of the eastern regions of the Peninsula over the last twenty centuries. Why mainly the eastern and not the western regions? We shall explain this after presenting a panoramic survey of the historical features of the character and outlook of the tribes inhabiting the eastern regions of the Arabian Peninsula, specifically the tribes of the hinterland, not the coastal areas.

A professor at the Department of Middle-Eastern Studies in a leading Western university confided, 'In most academic circles here in the United States, we take it for granted that the Arabs' hatred of the West is the result of the intrusion of Western powers into the lives of Arab peoples, beginning with the colonization of Algeria in 1830, Egypt in 1882, Morocco in 1912, and so on.' The hatred of the people of the region for colonialism is a healthy and legitimate phenomenon in itself; and does not by necessity mean hatred of all that is Western or of Western progress. In fact, countries with a rich heritage of civilization and history such as Egypt, Greater Syria and Iraq were able to combine a hatred of colonialism with a sincere admiration for progress, thus showing a true understanding of 'progress' as distinct from 'Westernization', and exhibiting a refined and enlightened social conscience. The alternative would have been to indiscriminately admire both colonialism and progress as one entity, which would have been a demeaning and humiliating phenomenon that could only lead to the death of many things that were held dear. However, it would be a mistake to assume that all countries in the region are the same. This applies to societies with a history rich in culture and civilization, places already mentioned, as well as others in the Arab West (Morocco, Tunisia, and Libya) and, to a lesser extent, the coastal regions of the Arabian Peninsula, the geo-political situation of which has rendered them more open to the outside world than those situated in nomadic fashion in the interior.

The harsh geopolitical conditions of the latter can only give rise to a rigid, inflexible and insular tribal mentality that refuses the 'Other' (whoever this 'Other' may be) in a xenophobic manner. The history of hatred of these desert communities toward anyone who differs from them in religion or thought is common knowledge; contrary to what some may think, this animosity is not a consequence of the Hanbali form of Islam (particularly Ibn Taymiyya's interpretation)[1] that they embrace; but rather, this rigid school that was categorically refused by the Muslim world at large could only find acceptance in this desolate region. Indeed, for more than a thousand years the ideas and edicts of Ibn Taymiyya with all their harshness, bigotry and hatred of non-Muslims found no adherents in Egypt, Syria and the Arab West, for how could the descendants of such highly evolved civilizations accept isolation from the rest of humankind?

A. Locked in the Inlands

For the past twenty centuries, the tribes living in the eastern regions of the Arabian Peninsula have been leading a pastoral as opposed to a settled life, roaming in search of pasturage and water. As a result of this lifestyle, the attitude of the Arab tribesman living in those regions towards such notions as loyalty, objectivity and neutrality cannot be understood in isolation from the sociology of nomadic life, the culture pattern of Bedouin tribes forced by their environment to move constantly in search of sustenance. Their unconditional loyalty is reserved for the *sheikh* (elder) of the tribe; objectivity is an alien concept and neutrality akin to treason.

As the eminent Egyptian critic Galal al-Ashri noted in his treatise on Arab creativity, the only creative area in which the Arabs excelled was poetry.[2] They did not produce drama, novels, epics, music or other creative forms like the Greeks and, prior to them, the Egyptians and the Sumerians. The poetry composed by the poets hailing from the eastern regions of the Arabian Peninsula is a mirror reflecting the value system of the tribes of the region, their mores, concerns, behaviour and thinking, and their devotion to the glorification of these tribal values.

The image reflected by their poetry has remained unchanged for centuries. An ode written in classical Arabic over ten centuries ago by a poet from Najd reflects the same values and world view as one written in the vernacular by a poet living in Najd today. Most of the poetry of the region, old and new, resounds with the cadence of stirring imagery, its main themes are pride and the superiority of the Bedouin who is always victorious, never defeated, who bows to no one and stands high above all others. In fact, the word for 'lofty' in Arabic is '*nuf*', from whence the proper names Nayaf, Nuf, and Nawaf are derived. This then is the message that thousands of odes by poets from Najd, Hasa, al-Qassim, and al-Hufuf have tried to convey ever since the Arabic language in its present form came into being and up to the present day. This view of life as reflected by the poetry of the region encapsulates the sociology of its nomadic tribes. The tribal Arab mentality formed in the inland deserts of the eastern Arabian Peninsula took over leadership of intellectual life in Arab and Muslim societies after the failure of the stage of liberalism, and the blend of socialism and Arab nationalism that had at one time held sway. However, the degree to which Arab and Muslim societies have come to be influenced by the tribal mentality born in the harsh eastern wasteland of the

Arabian Peninsula differs from one society to another in proportion to each society's historical and cultural legacy, and according to its political and socio-economic conditions. Thus, while its influence was most strongly felt in the inland regions of the Arabian Peninsula, it was weaker in the coastal cities of the Peninsula, and weaker still in societies such as Egypt, Morocco, Syria, Iraq and India that enjoy a richer legacy of history, civilization and culture than the Arabian Peninsula. Yet the Bedouin world view forged in the barren deserts of the eastern Arabian Peninsula and expressed in the poetry produced by poets from the region is the most important key to understanding the ways of thinking prevailing in many Arab and Muslim societies.

The cultural patterns that formed the Bedouin world view are in total contradiction with the concept of statehood. Loyalty to the *sheikh* of the tribe[3] is personal by its very nature, while loyalty to the state is a more abstract notion. In the tribe, obedience to the wishes and instructions of the *sheikh* is the counterpart of the modern citizen's adherence to the constitutional and legal rules of the state. According to the sociology of the tribal mentality, the specificity of which has been described in some detail here above, the 'Other' is perceived as an enemy or, at best, as a potential enemy to be neutralized. In the modern state system, on the other hand, the 'Other' is regarded as a natural expression of the diversity of life, inspiring neither rejection nor enmity. In a tribal environment, there can be no discussion of such issues as diversity, acceptance of the 'Other', engaging in self-criticism and accepting criticism, the universal nature of knowledge or the recognition that it is the collective legacy of humanity as a whole, all being fruits of the modern, progressive, civilized state. Indeed the very notion of humanity is alien to the tribal society.

If we borrow from the great fourteenth-century philosopher Ibn Khaldun's[4] theory on the distinction between urban and Bedouin societies,[5] we can say that the contemporary Islamic mentality (not Islam itself) is conditioned by a brand of Islam as understood, presented and propagated over the last half century by the Bedouin tribes living in the inland deserts of the eastern Arabian Peninsula. Given that most of the Islamic centres and schools established in North America, Europe, Australia and in non-Muslim regions of Asia and Africa were set up at the initiative, and with the funding of representatives of this insular tribal mentality, it is not hard to understand why the world today sees itself locked in a major confrontation between humanity and Islam. In truth, however, the confrontation is between humanity and a model of Islam which is presented, financed and propagated by the Bedouin, or Najdi, mentality.

The reason, then, to focus on the eastern inland areas of the Arabian Peninsula rather than on the eastern coastal areas and the region of Hejaz,[6] is that the inland areas were the crucible in which the brand of Islamist thinking known as Wahhabism was forged. The ideas of Wahhabism are typical of a superstructure (thought) born of a specific infrastructure (the geopolitical and economic features of the Najd desert); adherents to this view of the world cannot conceive that no other place on earth would have put up with such beliefs.

B. 'Blood, Blood, Destruction, Destruction'

The founder of Wahhabism, Muhammad Ibn Abd al-Wahhab, had laid down the broad outlines of his missionary design before 1798, a year which witnessed the first confrontation with the West in modern times, namely Napoleon's campaign into Egypt.[7] The first years of the fledgling Saudi state, soundly crushed by the Egyptian prince Ibrahim Pasha in 1818, and of the second Saudi state, which came to an end in 1891, were marked by an obdurate rejection of modernity and of all signs of modern civilization, combined with hatred of non-Muslims and indeed of all Muslims who did not follow the same tenets.

The Egyptian or Syrian Muslim who saw nothing wrong in singing, for example, was considered by the first and second Saudi states to be no better than an infidel. When the Brotherhood fought King Abd al-Aziz for allowing signs of modern civilization, such as the radio and the motor car, and foreigners into the kingdom, they were simply giving vent to the archaic tenets and beliefs of a system of jurisprudence that had no place in modern times and could have survived nowhere except in terrain whose geographic features imposed its isolation. Muhammad Ibn Abd al-Wahhab was by no means a jurist but merely a proselytizer seeking converts to the Najdi model of Islam.

When the alliance was forged between Muhammad Ibn Saud[8] and Muhammad Ibn Abd al-Wahhab, whereby the former agreed to rule according to the doctrine preached by the latter, a succinct statement was made by al-Wahhab shortly after the deal was struck; it expresses the essence of his doctrine, 'Blood, blood, destruction, destruction'.[9] These four simple words summarize what was and what continues to be the message of Wahhabism. The partnership between the two men led to the first incarnation of the Saudi-Wahhabi state.

The first Saudi state banned what it considered to be heretical practices, including the building of tombs, music, singing and dancing and any other manifestation of what they termed as un-Islamic conduct. Members of other faiths were hated and despised as 'unclean'. Such was the hatred of foreigners that European consultants brought in by King Abd al-Aziz at the beginning of the twentieth century were spat upon by the Ikhwan, members of an ultra-orthodox offshoot of the original Wahhabi movement. The presence of non-Muslims on the sacred ground of the Arabian Peninsula was seen as a desecration, as was any hint of modernity, even when it came to such trivial matters as the shape of beards and moustaches.

To the theologians of the first Saudi-Wahhabi state, the only rightful interpretation of Islam lay in the Hanbali school of law – founded by Ahmad Ibn Hanbal and further elaborated by his two main disciples, Ibn Taymiyya and Ibn Qayyim al-Jawziyya – even though it is by far the weakest of the four Sunni schools of law (Hanafi, Maliki, Shafi'i and Hanbali).

III. THE YOUNG SCION

Following Ibrahim Pasha's defeat of the first Saudi-Wahhabi state, the Saudis, with their Wahhabi partners, entered into an alliance with the al-Rashid family, who ruled the eastern region of the Arabian Peninsula from their capital Ha'il. The alliance between the Rashids – previously the Sauds fierce rivals – and the second Saudi state continued until the Rashids turned against the Saud family and sent them into exile in Kuwait in 1891.

In 1901, the young scion of the Saudi family, Abd al-Aziz son of Abd al-Rahman son of Faysal al-Saud, born in 1875 and endowed with the quality of leadership, seized Riyadh in a night-time raid. From 1902 until 1925 he waged a campaign to assert his dominion over the Arabian Peninsula and, after seizing Mecca then Medina in 1925, proclaimed himself the ruler of Najd and other provinces now known as the Kingdom of Saudi Arabia.

In the course of a historical journey that has no parallel in history, the actions, policies, words and deeds of Abd al-Aziz between 1902 and 1925 not only confirmed his exceptional leadership qualities but also bespoke a profound understanding of the nature of power, both in absolute terms and as exercised by the Great Powers, whether the Ottoman Empire, the British Empire, or the empire that was to emerge later, the American Empire. Abd al-Aziz Ibn Saud played his role with great skill, using all his acumen to achieve the goal he had set himself during the years of exile in Kuwait as the guest of the Sabah family in general, and of the ruler of Kuwait, Sheikh Mubarak al-Sabah, in particular.

Long before the Americans used the Islamists during the Cold War to help them defeat the Soviet Empire (notably after the Soviet invasion of Afghanistan in 1979), Abd al-Aziz Ibn Saud used Islamists to consolidate his own power. In 1912 he began and financed a movement known as the Ikhwan, a forerunner of the Islamist jihadists deployed by the Americans against the Soviets in Afghanistan. The symbiotic relationship between Abd al-Aziz and the Ikhwan ended in 1930 with a ferocious battle between the erstwhile allies, when the Saudis, led by King Abd al-Aziz, crushed the Ikhwan, led by Faysal al-Da'waysh.

The Ikhwan's religious views were so extreme that they considered any sign of modernity or progress the work of the Devil. As their alliance with Ibn Saud coincided with a period of great scientific advances, they had plenty of abominations to contend with: the telegraph, cars, telephones and radios were all regarded as sinful, and anyone who did not resist them was a heretic. Such was the fanaticism of this lunatic fringe that one of its members advanced on the Sultan (Abd al-Aziz Ibn Saud) with a pair of scissors and proceeded to shorten his robes in full view of his entourage, thereby driving home the message that the principles of Wahhabism were stronger than the authority of the Saudis. Apparently short robes are a basic tenet of Wahhabism, and failure to observe this essential requirement of orthodoxy is heresy!

Abd al-Aziz, first as prince, then sultan, then king, used the Ikhwan when he needed them to further expand his suzerainty. For like all those who welcome death as a passport to paradise, they were fearless fighters. The problem was that they were equally fearless in standing up to Abd al-Aziz whenever they considered him to have deviated from the true path. During the years of their increasingly uneasy alliance (from 1912 until he succeeded in asserting his dominion over most of the Arabian peninsula in 1925), fierce clashes often broke out between them. The sultan could not countenance any challenge to his authority as undisputed leader of most of the Arabian Peninsula. He barely had time to bask in the glow of his hard-won victory over the Hashemites and the expansion of his dominion over lands previously under their control before the Ikhwan forced his hand. They were routed, and their leader, Faysal al- Da'waysh, was captured and imprisoned, dying in captivity a few years later.

IV. THE SEQUEL

But the question is whether the Saudi state, successful though it may have been when it came to defeating its enemies, has been equally successful in ridding itself of the fanatical, not to say downright psychotic, ideas propounded by the Ikhwan of Najd, who militate against the use of cars, telegrams and radios and for the shortening of robes, the shaving of moustaches, and the growing of beards. The truth is that the Saudi state, whether in its first, second or third incarnations, has never been free of the pernicious effects of the doctrine preached by the Ikhwan. To this day, Saudi jurists remain committed to the version of Islam propounded by Ibn Hanbal, Ibn Taymiyya and Ibn-Qaiyim al-Jawziyya, even though they rank far lower in stature than such towering Islamic jurists as Abu Hanifa al-Nu'man, Malik Ibn Anas, Ja'far al-Sadiq, and Ibn Rushd (the second teacher after Aristotle).

Where jurists like Abu Hanifa and Ibn Rushd relied on the tools of rationality and deductive reasoning, compilation was the hallmark of the Hanbali School, which allowed no scope for reason or independent thinking but insisted on a dogmatic interpretation of holy texts. Thus, while Abu Hanifa relied on *istihsan* (preference of using few traditions and extracting from the Quran by reasoning the rulings which fitted his ideas) and Ibn Rushd on *ta'wil* (deductive reasoning), Ibn Hanbal insisted on a literal interpretation of holy texts. This led him to accept over ten thousand of the Prophet's hadith as apostolic precept. It also bred a climate which favoured unquestioning adherence to tradition over the use of critical faculties, creating generations of followers and imitators, and leading Islamic societies to the point at which they find themselves today: sidelined from history, science and the march of human progress.

The Hanbali School has turned the Muslim mentality into a passive recipient of answers instead of one that asks questions, let alone one that engages in critical thinking, the main engine of human progress. Although of all the Islamic jurists Ibn Hanbal was the most zealous proponent of orthodoxy and tradition, allowing little if any room for deductive reasoning, he was a product of his time. It was a time when the Islamic Empire was reeling from the onslaught of the Moguls and the Tatars,[10] and he cannot be blamed for ideas that were appropriate to the age in which he lived. The blame lies with those who, living in a different time and place, base their ideas on those of Ibn Hanbal.

A. Export of Hatred

Today, the Saudi state resists the education and employment of women, frowns upon television broadcasts, bans female drivers and considers music and singing sinful. The underlying logic behind these anomalies is not very different from that which informed one of the most heinous crimes in the history of Islam, the takeover of the Masjid al-Haram (the sacred mosque which is home to the Ka'ba) at the beginning of the fifteenth century of the Hijra calendar. All attest to the continued influence of Ikhwan ideas in the Kingdom, as do the ban on teaching music and philosophy in Saudi schools, and the refusal to appoint women to the Shura Council or in cabinet posts.

There is also the spate of *fatwas*[11] inspired by this madness, like the *fatwa* in which Ibn al-Baz, the grand mufti of Saudi Arabia from 1993 to 1999, concludes that the earth is not round but flat, and the one proscribing the sending of flowers to the sick! The reason that purchasing flowers to send to a sick person is *haram* (sinful) is because it is a custom that originated in the 'infidel countries'. This might seem trivial, but it is not, because it discloses a mentality that blindly rejects anything that comes from outside its own narrow confines. It also reveals the laughable contradictions inherent in this type of thought: sending flowers is declared a sin because 'it did not form part of the Islamic way over the centuries'! As if travelling by plane or car or using a computer – or indeed, using the sophisticated modern weapons that these people employ against their so-called enemies – were part of the 'Islamic way over the centuries'!

Any Muslim (outside the insular world of Ibn Taymiyya) would feel nothing but revulsion against the mentality that could spew forth this type of ruling – Edict No. 21409, dated 29/03/1421 (the Hijra year according to the Muslim calendar, 2000 by the Gregorian)

– and comprising terms such as 'This is but a custom that has come to us from the Infidel Countries and has been adopted by those of weak faith who have fallen under their influence ...' A mentality that fights flowers, the symbol of beauty, goodness, friendship, innocence and love across all cultures; flowers, the names of which in many languages denote a host of beautiful, uplifting meanings!

Only the narrow-minded mentality of these nomadic tribes could wish to turn Muslims into a culture of flower-haters! If this is the way these people view non-Muslims, it is no wonder that from time to time they should churn out warped individuals who indiscriminately open fire on the signs of modern civilization and on foreigners ('infidels') who are 'desecrating' the soil of the Arabian Peninsula (using weapons made by the said infidels!). To stop the madness, the Saudi establishment must take a firm stand, preferably accompanied by a psychological campaign.

During the second half of the twentieth century, the Kingdom of Saudi Arabia spent hundreds of billions of dollars to spread this doctrine, which had by then become influenced by three external factors: the ideas of Abu Ala al-Mawdudi, the Pakistani theologian /political philosopher who founded the Jama'at e-Islami party there; the Egyptian Muslim Brotherhood ideologue, Sayyid Qutb, and the Sururiyya school of the Muslim Brotherhood's Syrian chapter.

But these factors did not dilute the essence of the Wahhabi understanding of Islam. On the contrary, because of the simplistic thinking of Muhammad Ibn Abd al-Wahhab in comparison with the schools of al-Mawdudi, Qutb and the Sururiyya, these principles were the ones that most often were absorbed by the mass audience. Hence, these groups helped to reinforce it and swell the ranks of its adherents.

One of the most alarming developments of the last five decades is that the Najdi mentality spread to venerable Islamic institutions in countries like Egypt, Tunisia, Morocco and Syria, eroding their original features, and replacing them with its own. Thus while in the past we knew when listening to the Friday sermon in Egypt that the speaker was either a Shafi'i or a Hanafi, and in Morocco or Tunisia that he was a Maliki, we now hear an altogether different tune, a single Hanbali note set to the music of Ibn Taymiyya and Ibn Abd al-Wahhab.

B. Two Sides of One Coin

Despite all of this, there should be a distinction between Wahhabism as described above and the Saud royal family. Even though it entered into an alliance with the Wahhabis, it does not necessarily share their views. Indeed, the House of Saud has reached a watershed in its relationship with both the Wahhabi interpretation of Islam and the remnants of the Ikhwan. When it transpired that most of the criminals of the attacks on 11 September 2001 were Saudi nationals, the Saud family realized that it was time for a showdown. There is, after all, a historical precedent on which to draw, namely, the stand taken by the father of their oldest prince, King Abd al-Aziz Ibn Saud, who took on the Ikhwan and defeated it decisively.

V. THE INEVITABLE CHOICE

What is needed today is for modern, enlightened Saudis to realize that their problem lies primarily in addressing a distorted mentality that has no place in today's world – or indeed in any place or time. It is not fitting that they should have to live with the kind of edict that prohibits a woman from driving a car, for example. Indeed, there is no Quranic text that impedes Saudi Arabia from forming a new entity for jurisprudence that could select as its source far more enlightened and civilized schools than those of Ibn Taymiyya and Ibn Hanbal.

Such a programme for the House of Saud would include:

1. Resistance to extremist elements in the country.
2. Removal of Wahhabi and Ikhwan zealots from influential positions in educational institutions.
3. Removal of Wahhabi and Ikhwan zealots from influential positions in the Ministry of *Waqf*, (religious endowments), *da'wa* (the call to Islam), and *hajj*.
4. Abolition of the system of state-sponsored religious vigilantes like the *mutawa'in* and the *amr bel ma'ruf wal-nahi an al-munkar* – 'enjoining what is right and prohibiting what is wrong' – who patrol the streets and mete out instant punishment for any perceived violation of strict Islamic practices, in total contradiction with the concept of the modern state.
5. Reduction of the huge, $3 billion budget allocated by the Kingdom to the religious establishment and reallocation of it to the fields of education and health.
6. Encouragement of moderate professors of Islamic jurisprudence to set a timetable for introducing their students to Hanafi, Maliki

and Shafi'i sources in place of the Hanbali sources now exclusively in use so that, in time, the people of Saudi Arabia reach a stage of religious maturity in which they recognize that the doctrine of Wahhabism is not the only, or even the major, model of Islam.

7. The launching of an offensive against the Ikhwani obduracy on such issues as the appointment of female ministers, the inclusion of women in the Shura Council, allowing women to drive and allowing male teachers to teach female students and female teachers to teach male students, in order to promote a climate favourable to enlightenment and progress in place of the current reactionary climate that has no equivalent on earth.
8. A plan for the transformation of Islamic centres, established by Saudi Arabia throughout the world as a breeding ground for fanaticism and extremism and crucibles for violence, blood lust, and terrorism, into community service centres.

These opinions are motivated not by enmity for Saudi Arabia, but out of serious concern for its future. For unless the descendants of the great King Abd al-Aziz Ibn Saud follow the example he set with his stand against the Ikhwan of Najd eighty years ago, Saudi Arabia is headed for a highly detrimental confrontation with advanced societies. The collapse of the Saudi regime would represent a great strategic danger to all the countries of the Gulf and the Middle East.

NOTES

1. Taqi ad-Din Ahmad Ibn Taymiyah, *Al Tafsir Al Kamil* [The Complete Exegesis] (Beirut: Dar Al-Elfikr).
2. Galal Al-Ashri, *Thaqafatuna bayn al assala wal mu'assara* [Our Culture between Authenticity and Contemporariness] (Cairo: Al Hay'a Al-Misriya Al-'ama Lelkitab, 1981).
3. Eldest or chief of the tribe.
4. 1332–1406 AD. Arab Muslim polymath.
5. Abd Ar Rahman bin Muhammed Ibn Khaldun, The *Muqaddimah*, available at: http://www.muslimphilosophy.com/ik/Muqaddimah/Table_of_Contents.htm.
6. In the west of the Kingdom of Saudi Arabia.
7. The French campaign in Egypt lasted three years, from 1798 to 1801.
8. Ruler of Al Dar'iyah and son-in-law of Mohamed Ibn-Abdul Wahhab.
9. The Shia Newspaper No.2 available at www.shianewspaper.com/issues/no2/no2.pdf.
10. People who came from Asia and built an Empire beyond the continent.
11. A *fatwa* is a legal opinion or decree handed down by an Islamic religious leader.

6

The Other Side of the Coin

The Muslim Brotherhood was launched in 1928 to restore a caliphate, a global religious government aimed at fighting the 'non-believers' (specifically, Christians, Hindus and Jews) and at spreading Islam. The group opposed the existence of any secular states in all Muslim societies throughout the Middle East. The Brotherhood killed Egypt's Prime Minister Mahmud Fahmi Nuqrashi in 1948 and plotted to kill President Gamal Abdel Nasser in the early 1950s. An offshoot group, Islamic Jihad, led by Ayman al-Zawahiri, later Osama bin Laden's number-two man, assassinated Egyptian President Anwar Al-Sadat in 1981 and tried to kill President Hosni Mubarak in 1995.

I. THE MUSLIM BROTHERS' POLITICAL THOUGHT

The Brotherhood remains extremely opposed to Western civilization and to a political peaceful settlement to the Arab-Israeli conflict. Hamas is a Palestinian offshoot of the Muslim Brotherhood. This group's political thinking can be summarized as follows:

- *Political Freedoms:* Unlike Western democracies, which guarantee the political participation of every citizen regardless of ideology, opinion or religion, the Muslim Brothers make the political participation of individuals in society subject to the principles of Islamic Sharia.
- *Freedom of Belief:* The Muslim Brothers guarantee freedom of belief only for the followers of the three revealed (Abrahamic) religions, otherwise known as 'the people of the Book'.
- *Personal Freedoms:* While Western democracies guarantee the absolute freedom of the individual as long as it does not impinge on the freedom of others, the Muslim Brothers set freedom of thought within the strict parameters of a moral code derived from the Sharia. They call for the restoration of *hisbah*,[1] which allows a private citizen to prosecute any individual who commits

an act he considers a breach of the Sharia even if the plaintiff himself has not been personally injured by such an act. The right of *hisbah* was recently exercised by a private citizen in Egypt against the respected intellectual Dr Nasr Hamad Abu Zayd,[2] whose writings he considered as running counter to the teachings of Islam. The court ruled for the plaintiff, branding Dr Abu Zayd an apostate and ordering him to divorce his wife on the grounds that a Muslim woman cannot be married to an apostate. Dr Abu Zayd fled with his wife to the Netherlands.

- *Women's Rights:* In Western democracies, women enjoy the same political rights as men: they can hold public office and participate in political life without any restrictions based on gender. But as far as the Muslim Brothers are concerned, women's political participation would be limited to municipal elections; there is no question, for example, of a woman ever becoming head of state. To further marginalize women and exclude them from any meaningful role in public life, the Muslim Brothers call for educational curricula to include material that is appropriate for women, tailored to suit their nature and role, as perceived by them. In addition to special curricula for girls, they insist on a complete segregation of the sexes in the classrooms, in public transportation and in the workplace. The Islamist perception of women as lesser beings was illustrated in Kuwait, where Islamists temporarily blocked passage of a bill granting political rights to women.
- *The Economy:* The Muslim Brothers call for the establishment of an economic system based on the respect of private property. At the same time, however, they insist that it be based on the principles of Islamic Sharia, which criminalizes bank interest. They also call for state ownership of public utilities.
- *System of Government:* Contrary to the system of government applied in a democracy, which is based on the peaceful rotation of power through elections, the Muslim Brothers call for a system of government based on the principles of Sharia and the revival of the Islamic Caliphate.
- *Civil Society:* The freedom of movement enjoyed by civil society organizations in a democracy would, in an Islamist system, be conditional on their adherence to the strictures of Sharia.
- *Government:* The Muslim Brothers oppose the notion of a state based on democratic institutions, calling instead for an Islamic

government based on the *shura* (consultative assembly) system, veneration of the leader, and the investiture of a Supreme Guide. In this they are close to Iran's system.[3]

- *Political Freedoms:* While the legislative branch of government monitors the actions of the state to ensure that they conform to the rules of democracy, the actions of the state are monitored by the Muslim Brothers to ensure that they conform to the rules of Islamic Sharia.
- *The Arab-Israeli Conflict:* The Muslim Brothers were the first to send volunteers to fight Israel when it was founded in 1948. They have opposed all attempts to reach a peaceful resolution of the conflict, in particular the peace agreements between Egypt and Israel initiated by the late President Sadat. It would be true to say that the Muslim Brothers will never recognize the existence of Israel as legitimate.
- *Religious Minorities:* Although the Muslim Brothers of Egypt do not go as far as their counterparts in Saudi Arabia, where the construction of houses of worship for non-Muslims is prohibited, their position on the question of religious minorities includes the barring of any non-Muslim from becoming president and the subjection of non-Muslims to the principles of Sharia on which the entire legal system is based.
- *The Legal System:* The Muslim Brothers call for the establishment of a constitutional and legal system based on the principles of Sharia, including the application of corporal punishments in the penal code (stoning, lashing, cutting off the hands of thieves, etc.)
- *Violence against Civilians:* The Muslim Brothers have never condemned the use of violence against civilians, except if it is directed against Muslim civilians and even then only selectively.

Finally 'progress' in today's world is realized through the agency of science and effective business management, two areas of contemporary knowledge to which the Muslim Brothers have neither access nor commitment.

II. THE NECESSITY FOR DIALOGUE

Nevertheless, the harsh and often illegal treatment to which the Muslim Brotherhood is subjected is both unacceptable legally and self-defeating in that it hardens attitudes on both sides. In fact, the only way to resolve this problem with the Islamists is through dialogue, by opening channels of communication and engaging in a frank interchange of views. Debating the issues is the only way to transform a religious party, in the long term, into a civil political party that subscribes to the main tenets of democracy: acceptance of the 'Other', rotation of power, and respect for other religions and for women. The transformation will be complete when political Islam abandons its distorted understanding of our religion from one rooted in the Middle Ages and reflecting the mentality of Bedouins bred in a harsh and unforgiving desert environment. Civil society is entitled to protect itself from any group that remains locked in a time warp and would have us all retreat with it into a distant past.

Reform in Egypt is infinitely preferable to its takeover by any of a number of fundamentalist alternatives, as is reform in Saudi Arabia, where a coup by the fundamentalist tendencies could plunge the entire region into unprecedented chaos. Maintaining the stability of Saudi Arabia and of all its neighbours is imperative. But guaranteeing stability is impossible without a historical operation against the extremists. The question is whether the sane elements in Saudi Arabia will follow a course similar to the one taken by their famous forbearer eighty years ago or whether they will continue to attempt to coexist with them until the ship sinks with everyone on board.

III. THE REQUIREMENTS OF THE DIALOGUE

Dialogue with Islamists should be based on seeking the answers to the following questions:

1. Some of the Muslim Brothers (MBs) now expound the idea that Copts (Egyptian Christians) are 'fully first-class Egyptian citizens'. Would this imply that a Copt could be, in principle, elected president of Egypt?
2. Would the Muslim Brothers follow the Saudi model of segregating girls from boys in educational institutions such as schools and universities as well as all other organizations?
3. Tourism unrelated to history and culture (that is, 'beach tourism') now generates in excess of 75 per cent of Egypt's tourism revenues. What are the Brotherhood's views on the sale of alcoholic beverages, gambling and casinos, and women dressing in any way they choose?

4. What is the Brotherhood's opinion concerning the peace treaties between Egypt and Israel, and between Jordan and Israel?
5. What do the MBs think of the different forms of economic cooperation between Egypt and Israel – for example the Qualifying Industrial Zones [QIZ], in which joint enterprises receive special privileges for exporting goods to the United States?
6. How do the MBs describe the killing of Israeli civilians in Hamas or Islamic Jihad suicide operations?
7. Do the MBs believe that Sayyid Qutb's doctrine known as *al-Hak'imiyya* – that government must be based exclusively on Allah's law and which rejects democracy and human law as apostasy – is still the basis of their political system?
8. What are the views of the Brotherhood on women holding high government offices including ministries, the prime ministership and Supreme Court judgeships?
9. What are the group's views on the vision of a 'two state' solution for Israel and Palestine to live peacefully next to each other? Would they then accept and recognize the right of Israel to exist? Would they also accept that the Jewish section of Jerusalem is Israel's capital?
10. Egypt's legal system since 1883 has been based on the juridical notions of the European legal system. What are the Brotherhood's plans in this regard? And what do they think of physical punishments, such as the sanctions applicable in Saudi Arabia?
11. Like all modern societies, the Egyptian banking system is based on the notion of interests for lending and savings. Would the Brotherhood retain it?
12. Is Iran a factor of stability (or instability) in today's world?

Finally, one must know that the Brothers are likely to use *taqqiyya*, a principle which – according to clerics such as Ibn Hanbal and Ibn Taymiyya – allows Muslims to lie if so doing assists them in ultimately defeating the infidels!

NOTES

1. Based on a Quranic principle of enjoining what is right (good) and prohibiting what is wrong (evil).

2. 1943–July 2010. Egyptian liberal theologian who viewed the Quran as a religious mythical literary work; he was convicted for apostasy and heresy in the 1990s.
3. Established by Khomeini (1902–1989); it enables diehard conservatives – a group to which the Supreme Guide certainly belongs – to nip any process of reform or renewal in the bud.

Part II

A Confined and Barricaded Mentality

The wicked prowl *on every side,*
When vileness is exalted among the sons of men.

(Psalm 12)[1]

Introduction

Citizens unfortunate enough to live under oppressive regimes tend to be cut off from the influence of the outside world, and can associate modernity with the oppressions of former colonial dependence. Citizens such as these cannot conceive of democracy as their own human right, and not another form of oppression imposed by the West.

At a roundtable conference held in a centre for Middle Eastern studies in one of the United States' most prestigious universities, noted for bringing forth some of the world's most learned and respected names, a stimulating discussion took place concerning the so-called 'clash of civilizations'.[2] There were ten specialists attending the meeting, divided into two factions; those supporting the proposition that a clash of civilizations is an inexorable fact, as supported by the now famous assumption put forth by Samuel Huntington, and those who opposed this view. The latter formed a minority of only two persons, one of which was myself.

The general trend of the discussion seemed to be turning in favour of the former group with its insistence on the existence of this conflict, until one of the opposition put forth the following question: Japan was in a state of undeniable conflict with the free world until August 1945, the end of the Second World War. However, since then and up to the present moment, there has been no struggle or 'clash of civilizations' between Japan and the West, but only a vigorous economic, industrial, commercial and scientific competition played out according to the rules of the game as established by the free world.

If indeed a clash of civilizations had existed between Japan and the free world, the complete and impressive transformation that took place in that country in such a relatively short period of time could never have occurred. The salient point in this argument relates to the fact that when Japan was an autocracy, it was in constant conflict with the democratic world. This conflict ceased to exist once

Japan itself became a democracy, and it was replaced by the free play of commercial competition and cultural exchange, played out according to the rules of the game as practised by the free world.

It is not civilizations that clash, but rather autocracies and democracies that come into conflict. The Second World War was a war between autocratic and democratic factions; and so was the Cold War. This bears no relation to a clash of civilizations: no such thing exists.

While every Muslim community in the world has produced *jihadis* (fighters) for al-Qa'ida and other organizations, only one Muslim community has taken no part in this phenomenon. This Muslim community is the second largest in the world: the Muslim community in India. This community of more than 150 million people is the only Muslim community which does not have individuals who left the country to plan and take part in violent actions that are labelled by their perpetrators as *jihad*, which the rest of the world calls 'terrorism'. The Muslim community of India is not wealthy. It is part of Indian society, in which a high percentage of the people live a life far removed from wealth and prosperity. Nevertheless, this Muslim community has never produced a single individual who planned or carried out an action like the September 11 2001 attack in New York, or like the subsequent attacks in Madrid, London, Istanbul, Taba, Sharm al-Sheikh and other places. Moreover, the Muslim community in India (despite its minority status) produced a great scholar, who recently served as the president of his country.

Avul Pakir Jainulabdeen Abdul Kalam was the eleventh president of India, serving from 2002 to 2007. He initially worked in the Defence Research and Development Organisation (DRDO), made significant contributions to the development of India's first indigenous 'satellite launch vehicle' and conceived the Integrated Guided Missile Development Programme. As scientific advisor to the Indian government, Dr Kalam was responsible for the *Technology Vision 2020* documents, a road map for transforming India from 'Developing India' to 'Developed India'. He is known as 'the People's President' due to his unconventional working style, and as 'the Missile Man of India' for his work; he is regarded as a progressive mentor, innovator and visionary of India.

It is important to stress that the Muslim community in India is the only large Muslim community which lives in a genuine national democracy. What can we conclude from these facts? The obvious implication is that inside every individual on the face of the earth there is a political being. If this being finds overt, lawful and effective channels by which they can legitimately exercise their political ideals and aspirations, they will feel the need to pursue covert, underground political action.

India is not merely a democracy; it is the most populous democracy in the world. Not only has it managed to realize a great nation's dreams for a healthy democratic existence, but it has also enabled this nation to make significant progress in the spheres of economic development, scientific research, production, marketing and modern education. Moreover it handles the diversity of Indian society in a remarkable manner; indeed, the current prime minister, Manmohan Singh,[3] is a member of the Sikh minority which constitutes only 2 per cent of the population.[4]

The universities of India are rated among the finest in the world, while Cairo University, the most ancient university in the Arab world, does not rank among the world's 500 best universities.[5] The most important point is that India has proven that when Muslims, like any other human beings, exist in a healthy public climate that allows them full participation in political life, they do not turn to underground activities and are not driven to perpetrate terrorist outrages.

The reverse of India is evident in the allegiance of the Arabs to religion and to their rulers, an allegiance which blinds them from any other reality; they even lose sight of their own identity. This loss of identity locks them in an intellectual hostility which shuts them off from tolerance of the 'Other', and from the values of criticism; hence they ignore the meaning of 'compromise' and 'diversity', two essential elements of progress. The Arabs are thus confined to indulging in empty rhetorical discourse and self-praise, and live in the nostalgia for a past they have created in their own minds. Their lack of openness to the world renders them devoid of objectivity; they consequently become submerged by destructive beliefs such as conspiracy theories and the stereotypes they have created – making them hostile even to the minorities living on the same land.

NOTES

1. Author's translation from Arabic.
2. The Centre for Middle-Eastern Studies, Harvard University, 2005.
3. Manmohan Singh, born 1932; fourteenth and current prime minister of India since 2004,

he is the first Sikh (religious minority in India) to hold the position. He was previously minister responsible for the economy and initiated important reforms in 1991.

4. Based on the 2001 census the population groups are as follows: Hindu, 80.5 per cent; Muslim, 13.4 per cent; Christian, 2.3 per cent; Sikh, 1.9 per cent; other, 1.8 per cent; unspecified, 0.1 per cent.
5. Ranking Web of World universities available at http://www.webometrics.info/.

7

The Problematic of the Arab Mentality

I. BETWEEN VERBS AND DEEDS: A PSYCHOLOGICAL DILEMMA

If you are out to describe the truth, leave elegance to the tailor.
Albert Einstein[1]

The Arab people have been exposed to neither the Japanese nor the Indian models of democracy; and if the first shackle that enchained the Arab culture was an outdated, rigid and medieval interpretation of Islam, a second shackle was the natural consequence of a drastic deterioration in the educational system, media environment and cultural atmosphere, from which autocratic regimes can neither distance themselves nor claim innocence.

This enchainment has confined the Arabs to one vision of the reality of our world. Apart from fanatics who believe they are the keepers of absolute Truth and who do not for a moment doubt that their viewpoint is the only right one, most of us should have 'two persons' living within ourselves, each seeing matters from a different perspective. This is a healthy phenomenon, for doubt in all matters, more precisely doubt in our understanding of things, is one of the main engines of progress. Doubt is what drives the human race to constantly try and expand the horizons of knowledge, to learn and reassess its understanding in the light of the new knowledge it acquires, so as to attain ever greater intellectual maturity.

In my own case, for example, I often find myself pulled in opposite directions by the 'two persons' living within me. One is a man from the world of management who trained in a multinational corporation before attaining the top executive position in an international petroleum company whose culture derived in equal measures from its venerable European roots and from wide and lengthy international experience. The other is a man who indulged his insatiable appetite for knowledge from an early age; a voracious reader fascinated by the social sciences and the great masterpieces of human creativity.

Often, the ideas of these two people are contradictory, sometimes even confrontational. One issue on which they frequently clash is American and European policies toward the Middle East. While the intellectual is filled with admiration for European sophistication, the CEO is filled with anger at the ineffectiveness of European policies. The anger is compounded by his awareness of the economic interests and motives behind these policies. And while the intellectual within me despairs at the occasional lack of sophistication and misinformation on which American policies are based, the CEO believes that creative and decisive action can affect these policies and, ultimately, the American mentality in general. The intellectual aspires to a world order in which all decisions and actions are vested with international legitimacy; the CEO, on the other hand, deplores the inability of international legitimacy to act rapidly and effectively in nine-tenths of the cases.

When I lecture at universities and research centres in the United States, I sometimes find myself thinking that it is a pity that so much progress is not matched with an equivalent degree of sophistication; but when I lecture at similar institutions in France, I ask myself why so much sophistication remains in the realm of the abstract, why it is content to stop at couching elaborate ideas in beautiful language without translating them into effective and creative action. This is an attitude which seems to be incapable of acting, indeed, to not want to act in the first place, because many French, like many Arabs, have come to believe that sound can replace substance; that words speak louder than actions!

I know that many readers in the Arabic-speaking countries will be shocked when I say that if I am forced to choose between one of these two approaches, I would, without any reluctance, choose the American one. The reason is that the executive manager within would never forgive me for choosing the path of inaction rather than that of action. In his eyes, action, even if sometimes misguided, is preferable to the paralysis that has unfortunately come to characterize many French and Arab positions of late. At the same time, however, he is aware that decisive action can only produce positive results if undertaken by those who dream of a world governed by the rule of law, in which justice and stability prevail, and where every person on the face of the earth is entitled to strive for development and prosperity, and to enjoy freedom of belief without discrimination and oppression.

The ideal approach would be a blend of the American, French/European and Arab approaches, excluding the many negative aspects displayed by and inherent in each. Conscience dictates that I include the positive elements of the Israeli approach in the blend, even though I know this will offend many Arab readers. Of course, we would first have to remove from the Israeli approach the misconceptions from which it is suffering as a result of an ascendant right-wing trend fuelled by religious fanaticism. Actually, when it comes to fanaticism, Islamic fundamentalism has more than met its match in the extreme Jewish right wing. But because of Judaism's close ties with Western culture, Jewish extremism has managed to project a much less negative image than its Islamic counterpart, which is seen as (and actually is) primitive, detached from the age, and inimical to Western civilization.

If I were asked to list the approaches mentioned above in order of priority based on logic and pragmatism, I would rank them as follows:

- The ideal approach would be one that blends the advantages of the European approach with those of the American perspective, while avoiding all or most of their misconceptions.
- Next would be the American approach as it is, despite the many negative aspects in it.
- The European approach would follow as it is, despite the many negative aspects it has.
- At the bottom of the list would be the so-called Arab approach, which in fact does not exist. Can anyone claim that there is a coherent Arab position when it comes to relations with the outside world? To democracy, progress and modernity? To human rights or women's rights?

I placed the Arab approach last because it is in fact not an approach at all, but a mixture of emotions, excitability and confused thinking, characterized by an overwrought imagination that is totally divorced from reality, rooted in the past, and based on sectarian or ideological considerations in an age when the role of sectarianism and ideology is receding fast. In addition most Arab positions epitomize the misconceptions from which the contemporary Arab mentality suffers (for example, conformist thinking, overblown rhetoric, lack of objectivity, an unhealthy tendency to escape into the past in a nostalgic bid to recapture glories that are sometimes without any historical basis).

For any criticism levelled against US policies to be credible, the critic must prove that his criticism is meant to be constructive, not destructive. This can only be done by admitting at the outset that, despite the misconceptions in its policies, the United States is scientifically, technologically, militarily and economically the leading power in the world, and that it could not have attained and preserved such a position unless it was better qualified than others to occupy it. Moreover American society provides the best environment in which these abilities and talents can flourish and reach the goals to which they aspire and deserve. It is also important to add here that, while there is no perfect democracy anywhere, the political system in the United States comes closest to the ideal that any lover of democratic freedoms can hope for.

Even so the United States is far from perfect and much of what is going on in its political kitchen needs to be set right. The same applies to western Europe in general, and France in particular. The Arab citizen who admires some of the positions taken by France is unaware that their motivation has nothing to do with justice and integrity or righteous anger for the sake of Arab rights. For example, there were the extensive business dealings which France and Germany conducted with Saddam Hussein's Iraq, as well as the way in which, despite not backing the war, France demanded a share in the spoils of the war on Iraq in the form of reconstruction contracts. The Arab mentality, which remains isolated from the age and is the product of a culture of grandiloquent poetry invoking imaginary glories, is incapable of grasping reality in a sober, clear-headed, and unemotional manner. The millions of Arabs lamenting the fact that the world is now governed by a single superpower and grieving over the demise of the other superpower, the former Soviet Union, conveniently forget that the first two nations to recognize Israel were the United States and the former Soviet Union. They also forget that it was when the Soviet-Arab bond was at its strongest that they suffered the worst defeat in their history, and that they are still paying the price for what happened to them on 5 June 1967.

From a dispassionate reading of history, the pre-eminence enjoyed by the Roman Empire in the distant past, by the British Empire in a more recent past, and by the United States today did not come about by virtue of ideas or theories, but was the result of the imperatives of history, geopolitics and economics. It is thus as futile to object to America's supremacy in today's world as it was to object to Rome's in the ancient world. To protest against the inevitable is self-indulgent and naïve; a grave mistake that is made by the overwhelming majority of the Arab intelligentsia.

What the Arab mentality needs at this stage is a leadership that can reconcile it with the past (which was never as glorious as the nostalgic tales spun by over-active imaginations would have us believe) and the present (which is no worse than it was in previous times when other great powers prevailed). What this outlook needs, in short, is a leadership that can act as a catalyst to develop a more realistic agenda.

In asking themselves how they can change reality to fit their aspirations, the Arabs are banging their heads against a brick wall. What they should rather be asking is how they can find themselves a role in the context of that reality; for just as we cannot hope to change the fact that the sun inevitably rises in the east and never in the west, we cannot hope to change the reality of the world as we find it. The first step Arab societies should take toward being an active part of this reality is to recognize their vast misconceptions, then work to rectify them.

II. THE MISCONCEPTIONS OF THE (AVERAGE) CONTEMPORARY ARAB MENTALITY

The cultural misconceptions of the Arab mentality stem from three main sources. The first is the repressive climate prevailing throughout Arab societies, the second is a backward educational system that lags far behind modern educational systems, and the third is a mass-media apparatus operated by those responsible for the climate of political repression to serve their own interests. The following are the most obvious misconceptions from which the contemporary Arab mentality suffers:

- The adoption of standpoints on the basis of tribal or religious affiliations rather than on the basis of their coherence, validity or intrinsic value.
- The spread of the phenomenon of the personality cult in Arab societies, where the relationship with the ruler is not based on mutual respect and accountability, but rather on the excessive adulation, not to say deification, of the ruler.
- An ill-defined sense of national identity: is it Arab, Muslim, Asian, African or Mediterranean?

- A lack of intellectual hospitality.
- Limited tolerance for the 'Other'.
- Limited tolerance for criticism and the virtual absence of self-criticism.
- An aversion to the notion of compromise, which is deemed to be a form of capitulation and defeat.
- A culture that encourages conformity and discourages diversity.
- The prevalence of what I call the 'big-talk culture', in which overblown rhetoric is used to compensate for the appalling lack of concrete tangible achievements.
- A tendency to indulge in excessive self-praise and to glorify past achievements as a way of escaping our dismal reality.
- An unhealthy nostalgia for and escape into the past.
- Deep feelings of inequality with others in terms of results and achievements, which make for a sense of inadequacy that is sublimated into an exaggerated and unfounded pride.
- A lack of objectivity and the growth of individualism.
- Setting great store in conspiracy theories and believing that the Arabs are always the victims of heinous plots hatched against them by their enemies.
- A tendency to unquestioningly accept stereotypes at face value.
- A lack of respect for women and minorities.

The following chapters are an in-depth examination of each of these misconceptions (or defects?) which will demonstrate that they are actually all interrelated. The example of Egypt will be frequently given, as what applies to Egypt, to a great extent, applies to most of the Arab societies.

NOTE

1. 1879–1955. German physicist, renowned for his theory of relativity; winner of the Nobel Prize for Physics in 1921. See http://www.quotationspage.com/quote/3011.html.

8

The Blinding Effect of Allegiance

Foreign students of contemporary Egyptian affairs believe that there has been a marked decline in the civility of public discourse in recent years, particularly when two opposing points of view contend over an issue of public concern. An examination of the long-defunct magazine *Al-Kashkul*, a pro-monarchy political weekly, shows that the scurrilous language thought to be the product of the last few decades was already in use by the 1920s. But further readings of the political and cultural writings of the period reveal that, side by side with the unfortunate tendency to resort to name-calling and slander, there also existed a sophisticated debating style resembling that of the West.

When Taha Hussein (1889–1973) who, though blind, was the greatest Arab intellectual and writer of the twentieth century, published his controversial book on pre-Islamic poetry,[1] he came under attack from many critics. Some argued their case soberly, using civilized language and confining themselves to an objective critique of the book; but others stooped to unacceptable depths of calumny and personal attacks. Such attacks were also the style of a writer such as Mustapha Sadiq al-Rafay, a contemporary pioneer in Arab literature, whose book *Ala al-Safud* [On the Grill],[2] overstepped the bounds of decency in the virulent personal attack he directed at Abbas al-Aqqad[3] as part of the debate between traditionalists and the new generation fascinated by European philosophy and literature.

In other words, public discourse in Egypt used to be conducted along two tracks simultaneously: one track observed the rules of civility and objectivity, shunning the use of insulting language and personal attacks; the other belonged to the no-holds-barred school of writing, which had no compunctions about resorting to vilification and mud-slinging to discredit the opposite party.

During the last fifty years, the objective school of public debate has gradually lost ground to a defamatory style, based on hurling insults at the opponent, in which polemists find it easier to demonize those making the opposing point of view than to argue their own case on its merits. Numerous examples attest to the prevalence of this phenomenon in our cultural life today, in Egypt and other Arab societies, where differences of opinion over a specific issue are often expressed in the form of vituperative exchanges of accusations and personal insults rather than addressing the core of the arguments or content of the message.

Take the strident campaigns launched on a periodic basis by some papers which all too often degenerate from an objective discussion of the issue over which they were launched into an all-out war against the person holding the opposing viewpoint, whose personal integrity and morality are called into question and who is accused of all kinds of private and public wrongdoing. At first it seemed that this was because a public debate offers an ideal opportunity to give vent to the pent-up feelings of anger and frustration some harbour deriving from the many problems in our day-to-day life. Although this is certainly one factor behind the phenomenon, the real reason is a trend that has marked public discourse in this country for close on half a century.

In the last five decades, public life in Egypt was strongly influenced by two main realities. The first is that the regime which came to power in 1952 was extremely intolerant of any opposition, indeed even of the mildest criticism; from the beginning, the regime brooked no opposition. To crush dissidents it used all the apparatus of the state, including the media, which launched devastating campaigns against anyone who dared raise a voice against the regime. The other reality is that the strongest underground opposition movement in the country was the Muslim Brothers, a party that was, and still is, notoriously averse to the least hint of criticism, dealing with whoever refuses to toe the party line either with an iron fist or with floods of speeches and writings. Thus Egyptians, and Arabs more generally, have been caught between a ruling establishment that crushed its opponents with all the means at its disposal and an opposition movement that destroyed its opponents both materially and morally.

In such a climate of fascist intolerance where any divergent opinion was ruthlessly crushed whole generations grew with no knowledge of the rules of civilized debate and were raised to believe that opponents and critics were fair game for the most ferocious attacks on their probity and honour, and that personal insults and abusive language were entirely legitimate.

Attitudes like these cannot be conducive to the promotion of values such as tolerance of the 'Other', accepting constructive criticism, engaging in self-criticism, expanding the objective margin in thinking and debate or genuinely embracing pluralism. There have been a number of notable exceptions to this general rule, but these are unfortunately far outnumbered by the examples of oral and written debates conducted along fascist lines, which represent the dominant tendency in our public discourse at this time. It is a trend that is likely to remain dominant for some years to come, and until the process of economic reform now under way has been successfully completed.

Then the fundamental changes introduced into public life will make those who now feed the dictatorial trend mere relics of a bygone time, products of a stage which left its mark on the attitudes of some members of our society, until the new global changes divested them of their very raison d'être. However, this remains many years in the future and, in the meantime, we will continue to suffer from the trend that dominates public debate in Egypt and the rest of the Arab societies today; a trend that blurs our vision and confines us to a barricaded culture.

I. THE BARRICADE OF IDENTITY

A. The Cultural Barricade

With the collapse of the Soviet Bloc and the end of the Cold War, only one superpower remained on the world stage. This development opened new vistas before capitalist producers, who found an opportunity to conquer markets previously inaccessible to them. But first, new rules had to be set in place; rules that would reduce protectionism and open the field wide for competition, the mechanisms of which the capitalist producers were better equipped to deal with. It is from this reality that globalization was born.

Although essentially an economic phenomenon, globalization could only be envisaged in the context of wider interaction between different cultures, and it is this aspect of globalization, its cultural spill-over as it were, that many see as a greater threat than its purely economic aspect. Voices were raised against the globalization process and the danger it represents for specific cultural identities which, according to the anti-globalization lobby, are at risk of being altogether lost, or at best, greatly diluted in the context of globalization.

Actually, over the past forty years, an unfounded fear of cultural invasion has taken hold of the Arabs, permeating the thoughts of many in our society. Ever since the 1980s, with the division of the world into distinct 'Eastern' and 'Western' blocs coming to an end and the emergence of the concept of globalization, the issue of what is termed 'cultural globalization' has been extensively discussed in the region, with the fear being voiced that this global culture will overwhelm the Arab cultural specificity and annihilate it.

There is a panic in the hearts and minds of many members of the Arab communities concerning the possibility of losing their cultural identity. Yet only those with a modest store of cultural specificity are thus threatened. Countries with a vast cumulative legacy of cultural specificity, whose cultural identity is interwoven with historical and geographical factors, have little to fear.

Again consider the example of Japan, from which we could learn that such fear has its roots not in a threat emanating from the outside world, but rather from their own internal world of these fearful die-hards. Like the Japanese, the Arabs' cultural specificity is too deeply entrenched to waver. Those who describe the Japanese as having been culturally invaded by outside influences cite only inconsequential, culturally negligible phenomena such as eating fast food and wearing American-style clothing; however, human relationships, the veneration of elders, strong family ties, and the dedication to work which is quintessential to the Japanese culture, have all remained unchanged for the past sixty years, during which Japan has been actively and overwhelmingly exposed to dealings with the West.

Nevertheless, while it could be understandable that some might raise concerns over the Arabs' ability to maintain cultural specificity when confronted with the wave of globalization sweeping the world, the question of progress is a completely different matter. The principles and values underlying progress are completely in accordance with the principles upon which Arab cultural specificities are based: no one could possibly allege that the fundamental beliefs of Egyptians, Arabs, Muslims and Copts[4] conflict with concepts such as the value of time, dedication to work, the global nature of knowledge, teamwork, the culture of systems and of individuals and a firm conviction that management is a key tool to achieve success.

In fact I would have imagined that many of us would claim that these very principles were inherent in our history hundreds of years before they became the mainstay of present-day human civilization.

It might be thought that what I said applies to most of the values quintessential to progress, but is irrelevant where pluralism is concerned, for it is believed by some that Muslim religious thought is based upon one model of pure, absolute Truth; this, in my opinion, is a grave misconception. There are numerous texts in the Quran which support pluralism, the most significant of which is perhaps the text which points out that if God had wished all people to follow one single religion, then this would have occurred.

For instance verse 99 of *Surat Yunes* [10.99]: 'And if your Lord had pleased, surely all those who are in the earth would have believed, all of them; will you then force men till they become believers?' Or verse 35 of *Surat al-An'am* [6.35]: 'And if their turning away is hard on you, then if you can seek an opening (to go down) into the earth or a ladder (to ascend up) to heaven so that you should bring them a sign and if Allah had pleased He would certainly have gathered them all on guidance, therefore be not of the ignorant.'

Here is verse 48 of *Surat Al-Ma'ida* (Table) [5.48]:

> And We have revealed to you the Book with the truth, verifying what is before it of the Book and a guardian over it, therefore judge between them by what Allah has revealed, and do not follow their low desires (to turn away) from the truth that has come to you; for every one of you did We appoint a law and a way, and if Allah had pleased He would have made you (all) a single people, but that He might try you in what He gave you, therefore strive with one another to hasten to virtuous deeds; to Allah is your return, of all (of you), so He will let you know that in which you differed.

And, finally, verse 93 of *Surat al-Nahl* (Bee) [16.93]: 'And if Allah please He would certainly make you a single nation, but He causes to err whom He pleases and guides whom He pleases; and most certainly you will be questioned as to what you did.'

The *Sunna* (the traditions of the Prophet Mohammed) also abounds with texts that provide ample proof that pluralism is an inevitable fact of life.

It would indeed be strange to assume the existence of a conflict between our cultural specificities and between values such as respect for time or dedication to work; such an assumption simply propagates primitive, backward ideas. In fact, if additional proof were needed that the values of progress do not conflict with our cultural specificity, it would be sufficient to note that such values flourished in Egypt during the last century, and only dwindled at a later date, when what some people term 'the disintegration of the Egyptian society' occurred.

I remember when I was working for one of the most spectacularly progressive organizations in Southeast Asia in the 1980s, that it was generally held by most economic institutions in the area that there were two distinct work forces: the Chinese and the Malay. The prevailing belief was that for work to be done efficiently and well, it was best to rely on the Chinese, who were known for their dedication, good teamwork and strong work ethic. The Malays (who were Muslims) were, on the other hand, said to be lazy, inept slackers, with no respect for the work ethic. This belief prevailed until one man took over the leadership of a country where more than seventy per cent of the inhabitants were of the denomination categorized as 'ineffectual and unlikely to achieve'.

That country was Malaysia, where the population is predominantly Muslim. This leader was able to achieve a miracle, taking his nation to the highest levels of distinction in every field, so that in a period of less than twenty years, all the values of progress were manifest in this country which had previously been wallowing in a mire of laziness, ineffectuality and backwardness. The world thus discovered two major truths: First, that backwardness is not due to unalterable biological factors but rather to circumstances which, if changed, could reverse the situation completely. Second, progress can be planted and flourish in Christian, Buddhist or Muslim environments, and is not exclusive to anyone.

It is worth noting that all Malaysian cultural specificities pertaining to human relationships, family ties and religious values remained unchanged in this age of progress and did in no way diminish. To those who venture to say that this progress was brought about by the Chinese minority in the country, I would simply reply that this – if true – simply goes to prove that progress can be contagious, which is actually not a bad thing at all. However, to refute this theory in the case of Malaysia in particular is easy, for the simple reason that the Chinese minority had always been in Malaysia: what had been missing was the vision and the political will to allow the dynamics of the Chinese minority to be the catalyst or the locomotive of the Malaysian train.

The example of Malaysia explains why the interaction between the Arab mentality and Western culture is such an intriguing issue. Many public figures believe that valuing one's own non-Western culture implies hostility toward that of the West. Others believe that to be able to cope with the demands of modern life, one must be familiar with, and have knowledge of the Western culture – they often tend to ignore the Arabic Islamic culture in the process. A third group is disrespectful of Arab culture and has a disproportionate admiration for the alien Western culture. These stances are based on partiality and emotional bias, rather than on any awareness of or insight into the issues at hand. Even so most Egyptians, and Arabs in general, tend to lean toward one of these positions, and instead of adopting a confrontational attitude, such people should demonstrate that it is possible to assimilate elements of Western culture without becoming blindly attracted to it. We should not borrow concepts that could obliterate our identity as Arab Muslims.

Many intellectuals only have a superficial knowledge of noteworthy Arabic and Islamic literature. Most don't know the difference between Sharia (Islamic law) and *fiqh* (Islamic jurisprudence). They probably don't even know that the Islamic doctrine is a 'human' endeavour, subject to criticism and evolution. Blending law, jurisprudence and doctrine shackles enlightened thought, and it is a truism that one does not have the right to judge something one does not know. Those in the position to defend Arab culture are unable to do so because they don't know enough about it. Arabs and Muslims have every right to pride themselves on the enriching treasure trove that is our cultural legacy.

Quite frankly, the Arab mentality needs to undertake an honest process of self-examination and an unbiased contemplation of the following facts:

- Our cultural specificities include both positive and negative aspects.
- Our cultural specificities are not static but dynamic; those of the Egyptian people in the year 2000 differ in many respects (but not in all) from those of the year 1900, which were again different from those that had distinguished the Egyptians of the year 1800; those had also changed considerably since the year 1700. Accordingly, the widespread use of a term such as 'our fixed traits' is unscientific, imprecise and largely a figment of the imagination and of wishful thinking.

- Cultural specificities cannot be erased through widespread dealings with others, as amply proven by the Japanese. Indeed, the intrinsic identities of isolationists and those who shun the outside world are more likely to diminish, lacking as they do the stimulation and regeneration resulting from contact with others.

When the Arab mentality begins to contemplate the issue of widespread dealings with the 'Other' – in particular, joining the march of human progress together with the rest of the civilized world – it raises the now familiar cry, 'Our cultural specificities are in danger!' This fails to take into account the difference between integration with the outside world by playing the game according to the rules set by the advanced world and between a total assimilation that erases identity and cultural specificity. Brazilians play football by following the rules of the game, but in their own, very distinctive way, and in a manner that is theirs alone. Again the Japanese provide the best example of the validity of this argument.

As a matter of fact, even Arabs amongst themselves do not have the same cultural identity. Consider the case of Egypt: during the first four decades of the twentieth century, Egypt was inextricably linked with the Mediterranean. The Middle-Eastern identity was coined and cooked up in the 'kitchen of politics' and not in the 'kitchen of history'. Egypt's cultural dimension is deeply rooted in our geographical situation. The cultural leanness that has set in during the last few years and the recalcitrance of some intellectual trends has probably played a significant role in sapping this aspect of Egyptian life.

This dimension, however, is a significant bridge between us and the entire world and one of the distinctive characteristics of our civilization. Egyptians are culturally Arabs but certainly not in absolute terms; they are also eastern Mediterranean but not in absolute terms. And though they are part of the Islamic civilization, this is not their unique identity. Then too there are important Ancient Egyptian and Coptic components in their makeup. For example, although there is a great resemblance between Egyptian cultural mores and those of the Arabian Peninsula, they are not identical. The same can be said with regard to Egypt's Islamic and Mediterranean dimensions. For despite the importance of the Islamic dimension, it has not turned Egyptians into exact replicas of Indians or Indonesians.

In other words, the Egyptian identity is a compound one, a

multi-layered tapestry woven with a rich diversity of strands that are rooted in history and geography. Because the Egyptian identity is not the product of transient factors but has distant roots in both time and space, its specificity cannot be obliterated by the new phenomena that characterize the realities of the present.[5]

To understand the role of history and geography in forming the multi-layered Egyptian identity is to realize the complexity of that identity, and the depth of the overlapping layers of which it is constituted. Once this realization sets in, the dire predictions we are now hearing about the adverse impact that globalization will have on our cultural specificity and about how the new openness onto the outside world threatens the integrity of the Egyptian identity, will appear to be totally unfounded and illogical.

It would be wrong to suppose, however, that because an identity is complex, it remains static. The main components of identity are history and geography. The first is in perpetual motion, the latter, though apparently motionless, is in a state of suspended animation. The inevitable conclusion to be drawn from this is that the traits of any specific cultural profile are in a state of constant, albeit slow change, like 'time' itself, which is a dynamic process in a state of continuous flux. Thus the cultural specifics of an Egyptian individual living at the dawn of the twenty-first century are different from those displayed by his ancestors at the turn of the nineteenth century, which were in turn different from those displayed by our forefathers at the dawn of the sixteenth century.

If it is illogical to claim that our distinctive cultural profile has remained unchanged throughout the ages, it is equally unreasonable to claim that the traits of which it is composed are all positive. The best proof that negative strands are interwoven with the positive strands making up the tapestry of our cultural identity can be found in our popular sayings which celebrate the positive and decry the negative traits of the Egyptian character.

Those who fear that cultural specificity will be crushed under the weight of others from more powerful and advanced parts of the world would do well to study the case of Japan and other East Asian nations. Although these have dealt extensively with Western civilization, emulating many of its patterns of work and study, their cultural specificity has remained intact. Indeed, some of the more positive cultural patterns they assimilated from Western civilization and adapted to suit their own realities, like teamwork, have given them an edge in their dealings with the West. A short train journey from Tokyo to any other town in Japan attests to the undiminished vigour of Japan's cultural specificity, despite its extensive dealings with and opening onto a world having its own, distinct, and very different cultural heritage.

A number of questions need to be posed to those who dread the loss of cultural identity: Is American culture really capable of uprooting our cultural specificity and replacing it with its own? And, if American culture can obliterate the Egyptian identity, why couldn't British culture (which is deeper and richer than the American) obliterate India's cultural specificity over four centuries of British occupation? Why does the hamburger and Coca-Cola culture strike such terror in their hearts?

Finally, if it is impossible for America to assimilate us culturally, how can some people believe that Jewish culture can subsume our cultural specificity under its own? Egyptian cultural specificity is the result of a historical and cultural continuum stretching over seventy centuries, while Jewish culture has been exposed to many disruptions through the ages. Moreover, Jewish culture is practised by a small number of people in the world. If anything, it is the Jews who should – and probably do – fear that once peace is achieved in the region, their specificity will be exposed to a cultural onslaught from the surrounding cultures, especially that much of their cultural specificity stems from a ghetto mentality. Peace will mean the end of the ghetto and, with it, of one half of Jewish cultural specificity.

The lessons of history prove that societies which opt for opening onto the outside world, which interact with other cultures, help keep their own cultural specificity intact while promoting its development. There is also ample historical evidence to show that the total or partial isolation which some believe can protect their cultural specificity from erosion is likely to do just the opposite. Throughout the first half of the twentieth century, thousands of Egyptians were open to Western life and culture without giving up any of their own cultural specificity. In fact, their interaction with another culture enriched them by adding new elements to their own that boosted its positive attributes and helped correct some of its negative aspects.

B. The Intellectual Barricade

In the 1960s the prevailing cultural climate allowed unfettered access to world literature. Two factors were instrumental in creating this climate: the existence of a strong school of literary criticism, and an equally strong translation movement with its fountainhead in Lebanon. From the former we learnt which classics of world literature we should read, while the latter made those works available to us in our mother tongue when our mastery of European languages was inadequate to capture the richness of this human legacy.

The leading critics of the 1960s, such as Muhammad Mandur and Louis 'Awad, Abd al-Qadir al-Qutt and Raja al-Naqqash, served as our navigators through the uncharted waters of European culture, guiding us in our choice of reading material not only in the field of literature but also in Western philosophy, history, political economy, psychology, sociology and so on. Other luminaries included the philosophers and intellectuals Abd al-Rahman Badawi, Yussuf Murad, Zaki Naguib Mahmud and Murad Wahba.

At that time, it never occurred to any of those of my generation who loved knowledge and culture to question the nationality of what we read. We devoured the works of the Egyptian novelist Naguib Mahfuz, the Egyptian playwright and author Yussuf Idris, the Iraqi poet Badr Shakir al-Sayyab, the Syrian poet Nizar Qabbani, the Egyptian poet and writer Ahmad Abd al-Mu'ati Hegazi, the Egyptian pioneer of modern Arab poetry Sialah Abd al-Sabur, the Lebanese poet, novelist and translator Suhail Idris, the prolific Algerian writer Muhammad Dib, and the Egyptian writer and modern literary movement pioneer Yehia Hakki, as fervently as we did those of the countless foreign authors, poets and playwrights. It was never relevant to us that Yussuf Idris was Egyptian, that Suhail Idris was Lebanese, Muhammad Dib Algerian, Eugene Ionesco Romanian, that Graham Greene was English, Albert Camus French, Alberto Moravia Italian, that Henryk Ibsen was Norwegian, or that Eugene O'Neill was American. The issue simply did not arise because we had been raised in a cultural climate in which creativity was presented to us as the ultimate expression of human genius, its fruits being part of the common legacy of humanity taken as a whole. Egypt was still unsullied by chauvinism, or by the fear of the jingoistic expression, 'cultural invasion', that was beginning to rear its ugly head in the late 1960s.

Unfortunately the irresponsible use of this distasteful expression by some fell on willing ears, coinciding with the emergence of a regressive trend that was not affecting intellectuals in the 1960s: the new theory of cultural invasion began to take over, as Egypt fell prey to regressive ideas which were totally incompatible with the age and which rejected the notion that human civilization is an amalgam of many different civilizations and cultures. The numbers of those who subscribed to the cultural invasion theory continued to swell.

In the latter half of the 1970s, the tremendous decline in educational and cultural standards began; it further promulgated the idea that we were the targets of a cultural invasion. In a misguided attempt to resist the 'invasion' without foregoing any of the benefits of Western civilization, some of the theory's proponents came forward with the absurd idea that Western civilization could be broken down into two distinct components: a material component, represented in the applied sciences, technology, machinery and equipment, and a moral component – culture, art and ideas. They proposed that we adopt from the West only the material component and discard the rest. However, they overlooked two important issues:

1. That the material component of Western civilization is the natural result of its non-material, that is, cultural, component: 'Western civilization' began with ideas, art and literature; it was only after these had created a climate in which creativity could flourish that the applied sciences could produce their successive inventions and discoveries.
2. That 'Western civilization' is not exclusively European and American, but that it is made up of two elements, one derived from the cumulative experience of other civilizations and cultures, the other from the experience built up in a purely Western context. In other words, it has a dimension attributable to humanity in general, being the product of the civilization process experienced by all humankind, and a Western dimension linked to the history of western Europe from the late Middle Ages and the onset of the Renaissance.

Every effort must now be made to ensure that the current as well as future generations understand that the fruits of human creativity and endeavour are humanity's public domain, and that partaking of those fruits in no way represents a surrender of our specificity. They must be encouraged to emulate the example of a whole generation of Egyptians – Lutfi al-Sayyed, (1872–1963), an Egyptian intellectual known for his anti-colonial activism and also the reform rector of Cairo University; Taha Husayn; Ahmad Amin (1886–1954), Egyptian author and historian; Abbas al-Aqqad; Tawfik al-Hakim

(1898–1989), prominent Egyptian writer and playwright; and Naguib Mahfuz, who all remained ardently Egyptian despite their extensive forays into world culture and their profound appreciation of its masterpieces.

Mahfuz, widely considered the father of the modern Arabic novel and the only Arab Nobel Prize Laureate, does not hesitate to criticize aspects of Egyptian society or to adopt unpopular or defiant standings, such as his support for Salman Rushdie's *Satanic Verses*[6] or his objection to the Muslim fundamentalists in Egypt, which caused an attempt on his life. Yet, like his peers, his passion for Arabic literature and culture remained resolute.

Moreover it is materially impossible for any society today to lock itself into total or even partial isolation. The globalization of science and technology and the information and communication revolution are not only a bar to economic and cultural protectionism, but also render dreams of isolation both impracticable and unattainable.

Finally, the axiom that 'man is afraid of what he does not know' is perfectly applicable to those who fear the disappearance of their cultural specificity if they engage in extensive dealings with the outside world. If these proponents of isolationism had a better understanding of the multifarious strands that have converged to produce our specific cultural identity, as well as a wider knowledge of other cultures, they would not have the feeling of inferiority that makes them fear the loss of their own identity. Ignorance breeds a sense of inferiority, which in turn leads to a paranoid fear that the other is intent on destroying our identity. There can be no greater feeling of inferiority, compounded by a superficial and simplistic understanding of reality, than that manifested in the fear that exposure to other cultures will lead to the erosion of our own. To believe that our cultural identity will collapse when exposed to other cultures is an insult to our culture and civilization; for the underlying assumption is that our cultural specificity is so weak, that it cannot stand up to the challenge of other cultures if we open up onto the outside world, and that it can only survive behind high walls separating our culture from others, thus breeding intellectual hostility.

II. REPELLING DIVERSITY

The deplorable state of the Arab intelligentsia today can only evoke a feeling of sorrow within the hearts of those who wish to see the region receive its fair share of progress and development. These 'thinkers' are occupied with denouncing the rules of the game developed by the Western democracies, while propounding the theory that it is feasible to invent new rules for that game. It is a stance that is shared by no other countries, even those who might have been expected to show animosity to Western civilization, such as Japan and the stars of Asian progress, South Korea, Singapore, Taiwan, and, to a lesser extent, Malaysia and Indonesia.[7]

Standing at the beginning of the twenty-first century the Arab societies need to generate a cultural reconciliation between what is 'human', in the broad sense of the word, and what is 'specific'. If the will is there, such reconciliation is not only feasible but perhaps even easily attained, and this will provide a better and more effective stage from which to deal with the requirements and challenges of the age, locally and globally.

So far, this will is absent. In Egypt, for example, myriad reasons accumulate to make most of the modern citizens heavily imbued with the parochial, inward-looking attitude, which simultaneously deprives them of the wider, universalizing influences. On the one hand, citizens of ancient societies suffered a lot from foundering in 'localism.' The 'World' for them was first and foremost their homeland; hence the Egyptian saying, 'Egypt is the mother of the World.' On the other hand, throughout the 1960s and the 1970s we were being drowned in the parochial attitudes which cut us off from communication with the outside world. It is noteworthy that everywhere else this era was the time when, for the rest of the globe, the communications revolution brought the downfall of separateness caused by the isolating barriers between nations and people – hence, the starting point of the extension of mass media beyond nations' borders, with economy following the same course.

Furthermore, the educational curricula had incessantly concentrated on the national agenda (local history, civilization and literature) in a way contradicting, for example, education programmes in France where the curricula show great interest in the history of ancient Egypt, China and Greco-Roman civilizations, and which did not diminish the attention given to topics based in French culture and history.

In addition, for many years, the fact that the mass media and local press were both not much more than mouthpieces for the government also severely restricted their content to the nationalist agenda. The discrepancy between our news bulletins and those in many other countries is evidence enough: local news dominated, while by contrast coverage in the rest of the world followed events wherever they transpired. The growth of the relatively backward ideology in our society had been a grand triumph for 'localism' at the expense of 'universality'. This takes place within the spheres of the economy, culture, education and the media. Consequently our negligence of the necessity and significance of assiduous scientific research to achieve balance formulae between (localism) and (universality) might make us unable to deal, effectively and positively, with the mechanisms of the new era of globalization.

I have argued elsewhere that 'the engine' on which institutes, firms and societies rely on is 'efficient management'. I add – in this respect – that the 'management' (in our case 'bureaucracy') that founders in localism is too crippled to play the game of the future successfully. The basis of this contest is twofold: first, effective management (that is, profitable leadership); and second, comprehensive knowledge of the substance of the competitive process on the international level.

This applies to the economic as well as political aspects of societies' futurity. The Arabic-speaking people must therefore detach themselves from their hostility and intolerance to all that is not 'local'.

NOTES

1. Taha Hussein, *Fil Shi'r al Jahili* [On *Jahili* Poetry] (1926), available at: http://www.scribd.com/doc/2288049/.
2. *'Ala al-safud* was a collection of articles that comprised the author's very harsh criticism of the views and writings of Abbas al Aqqad (1889–1964) that were essentially the old Islamic camp fighting the new generation fascinated by European philosophy and literature, that is, the old stoning the new. See, for example, *Al Jozoor*, vol. 17 (Beirut: 2004), see *'Ala al-Safud* (Beirut: Dar al Kutub al 'Ilmiyah, 2001).
3. 1889–1964. Largely self-educated Egyptian writer, historian, poet, philosopher, translator and journalist.
4. The majority of the Christians in Egypt, of pure Egyptian descent.
5. See the work of Nobel Prize-winning economist, Amartya Sen, *Identity and Violence: The Illusion of Destiny (Issues of Our Time)* on issues of multiple simultaneous identities.
6. The novel, first published in 1988, whose British–Indian author, (Sir) Salman Rushdie (born in 1947) was threatened with death because the content of his novel was considered offensive to the Prophet. The then Supreme Leader of Iran, Ayatollah Khomeini, issued a religious edict (*fatwa*) calling for Rushdie's death. The latter lived in hiding for close to a decade.

7. It is my belief that Malaysia will soon catch up with the Japanese example after ridding itself of a leader who, while enjoying a high degree of administrative skill, is nevertheless a dictator who thinks nothing of imprisoning his opponents (after fabricating false accusations), and who recently joined the ranks of the defenders of Saddam Hussein.

9

The Absence of Tolerance and Critical Mind

I. THE VIRTUES OF TOLERANCE

The human being has a natural propensity to be highly-strung, and to reject – even be hostile to – those who differ, whether in religion, race, culture or social organization. Throughout different eras, this discrepancy – not to mention differing self-interests – fuelled conflict time and again.

But in the course of human development, a more tolerant and accepting attitude began to prevail, by which coexistence with the 'Other' became possible. The evolution of urban existence increased this acceptance, and to simply blame an individual for being different was not a mark of humanity but of barbarism.

Islamic civilization had been relatively superior to other old civilizations in its tolerance for others; the contrast between the behaviour of 'Muslims' and 'Christians' throughout the medieval period clearly demonstrates this. On the other hand, under the umbrella of Islamic sovereignty, the life of Christians and Jews was close to normal. Muslims, by contrast, had been exposed to persecution and uncouth torture after the exodus of Arabs from Spain; they were confined to ghettos as if they carried a contagious disease.

It is worth mentioning that as the Jews and Christians of Palestine, Syria, Lebanon, Iraq and Egypt lived under the banner of Ottoman sovereignty,[1] it would have been very easy to treat them as the Christians had dealt with Muslims in Andalusia when Muslim sovereignty declined there.

As to the modern age, tolerance – that is acceptance of the others' dissimilarity in respect of religion, race, traditions, sacred precincts and conventions – was, and will always be, primarily a phenomenon of culture. The more a society is saturated with education and culture, the greater the tolerance of its members toward others, and the more their acceptance of the fact that diversity among people is quite normal, and should develop tranquil co-existence!

Western civilization had been marked by racial fanaticism; the boom and prosperity of the West made people more tolerant. It is sufficient to cite the radical transformation in Europe's stance on the Palestinian issue during the last fifty years. Israel is nowadays no longer aided or supported by Europe, as was the case in 1948; increased cultural awareness has encouraged most Europeans to approve of the legitimacy of the Palestinian right, as they witnessed Israel behaving hypocritically. If it had not been for the cultural awareness of these European countries, they would have been condemned to their erroneous positions of the past.

But in the Middle East we must confess that the levels of tolerance have been spectacularly receding and shrinking during the last decades. Roughly half a century ago, the general cultural climate was freighted with developed human values firmly rooted in our hearts, and particularly in the hearts of those in the stratum leading the people culturally and intellectually. Dissimilarity was a mode of life, a landmark of human existence on earth. This cultural climate was far from 'the intellectual formula' that eventually developed, and which encouraged people to discriminate unfavourably between 'us' and 'them'. This formula can be described at the very least as:

- Inhumane and hostile, standing in complete intellectual contradiction with contemporary scientific and cultural values.
- Provocative, in that pursuit of this formula does not lead to peaceful coexistence with others, but to confrontation and contrariety.
- It is a formula that does not accord with the profound spirit of peace and humanity cherished by profound religious doctrines, whether Muslim or Christian.

Fifty years ago, tolerance prevailed, due to the cultural milieu. Yet this status quo suffered a defeat which unsettled the culture of tolerance. On the morning of 5 June 1967, the collapse of an entire political order was revealed, and so were clear signs of failure to manage our economy in the following years; those were followed by a serious rift in social cohesion. When these various manifestations became evident, some people totally estranged from the spirit of tolerant, cultivated values thought that their arguments were the best; and the status quo permitted them to wage propaganda for their views, which had not a jot of intellectual tolerance!

It is imperative to try to reform culturally this perilous defect that distorts our modern mentalities by taking a firm position toward what is the essence of the problem, namely that we are nowadays less tolerant and more fanatical about our faiths. We have never dealt with this defect, substantially or scientifically; this widens the gap between us and the rest of the world, especially those societies that are following the path of progress.

Additionally there is a deeply entrenched relationship between this recession of tolerance and another blemish, namely the bizarre belief in conspiracy theories. These two misconceptions will trap us in strict isolation from the outside world, and especially from the developments which are economically, culturally and strategically important.

Growth in the belief in conspiracy theories since June 1967, annexed to the recession of tolerance, rendered any mutual understanding or dialogue totally inexistent with the influential powers in the outside world. Simultaneously it gave historical enemies a situation much superior to ours in the eyes of these powers, and has a deleterious effect on internal dialogue, which also suffers from a lack of tolerance.

Undoubtedly educational institutions, mass media and all cultural institutions are a powerful means of opposing this lethal defect in the attitudes of the great majority of people. Unfortunately, any success in tackling such a flaw is extremely difficult; the yield of any effective reform in this domain becomes apparent only after years. All reforms in education, mass media and culture are long-term investments, with results that are guaranteed, profitable and effective only in the long run. Besides, there is no alternative.

II. TOLERANCE AND THE DYNAMICS OF CRITICISM

'Tolerance' is not limited to acceptance of the 'Other'; it also shapes the mentality to be flexible when this is required. It is necessary to stop denying one's own misconceptions, and turn away from hostility to all that comes from elsewhere; this cannot be done if there is no tolerance for criticism.

Criticism is a tool that every human being in the advanced societies acquires from the dawn of consciousness; the atmosphere in which people live in these cultures enables them to voice opinions and make criticism from the very start. The little child is taught how everything is subject to criticism; at the same time individuals practise criticism in an atmosphere of general acceptance and forbearance, remote from the wrath and stress caused by criticism in other cultural milieus, such as in many Middle Eastern societies.

Educational curricula consolidate this critical attitude, and the culture at large encourages constructive criticism, while by contrast, Arab culture has tended to react with hostility toward criticism, especially criticism of fundamental issues. Arabs, in many respects, regard criticism as sabotage and a destructive act of treason or betrayal, and seldom criticize in a calm, objective and polite spirit. Intolerance to criticism is deeply entrenched in Arab society. Other negative aspects are disseminated in their contemporary thought and make the issue extremely acrid. When intolerance to criticism is annexed to low levels of leniency and high levels of subjectivity, narrow-mindedness – reading others as either 'with' or 'against' them – together with fanaticism or phobia about the past and overweening inclination to self-praise, the intensity of intolerance to criticism reaches its zenith. Criticism becomes synonymous with wrath, anxiety and suspicion, added to the existence of perils lying in ambush to complete the plot against them.

The general atmosphere in Arab societies suffers a great deal from this intolerance to criticism. During the last few decades, many stereotyped cases were repeated, symbolizing this phenomenon as a characteristic in myriad intellectuals and cultural figures. This reaches extreme levels. For example, when some called for celebrating the two-century long relationship between Egypt and France, polemicists attacked and slandered them for proposing such a thing. The same applies to those who believe in holding negotiations or dialogue with Israel as the only way to escape from a terrible situation.

Thus there is a lack of the 'critical mind', apart from the meagre margin of democracy that is permitted, and the fact that top positions are often concentrated in the hands of a few incompetent individuals whose intellectual capacities and management skills are mediocre at best. When added to this is the current proliferation of a reactionary religious culture, it is understandable that there should be a marked decrease in rationality, a lack of participation marked by extreme negativity, and a prevalence of constants and fixed ideas that cannot hope to hold up against the objective criticism that is crucial to true development. This lack of democracy actively hinders social mobility, resulting in a general state of incompetence which in turn leads to a decline of standards at all levels. Invariably, rational thinking takes a back seat. Throughout the last thirty years, the mass media have been void of any article or interview including constructive criticism of current government's major choices or decisions. This is evidence of a choice between slogans and harangues.

A glance at many articles published in leading Egyptian daily papers that are written by a number of well-known Islamists would make us understand the reason for the Arab people's decline and their regrettable state of regression. When reputed newspapers with a wide national circulation allow what amounts to a demolition force against the values of humanity, civilization and progress, there is little wonder at the giant steps backwards being taken at a frightening speed. The articles bemoaned a glorious past that actually never existed outside the writer's imagination, and which was in reality characterized by excessive bloodshed and slaughter, which tended to be the norm all over the world at that time.

Writers develop endless tirades against the 'Other' who was pictured quite simply as the devil; and, in true tribal fashion, they persisted in seeing this 'Other' as a vile enemy intent upon destroying their society, and who therefore was to be fought against with words and the sword. This kind of 'reasoning' is typical of the desert culture, characterized as it is by tribal values, isolation and imaginary or real dangers lurking behind every dune. In actual fact, the 'Other' is neither devil nor angel; and based upon this premise, a constructive interchange of ideas and discussions can only benefit both sides and further the cause of progress and of humanity at large. This said, though, it should be remembered that the concept of 'humanity' is completely alien to the nomadic tribal mentality.

The 'Other' has played a significant and enriching role in our lives during the past two centuries, and has had a profound and positive influence on journalism, theatre, literature, translation and intellectual life and activities in general. Egypt was a melting-pot blending the Egyptian with the 'Other' in a harmonious and productive fusion which resulted in countless works of beauty, refinement and cultural merit. Isolation, on the other hand, has spawned a decline in aesthetic values and an ugliness that few can deny. It must be hoped that the minorities in Arabic-speaking countries will serve as a catalyst for the dissemination of progress and refinement, taking society forward toward the time we live in, rather than backward to a past that belongs to the Dark Ages.

In addition 'Total Quality Management' (TQM) is the main cause of the success of any economic activity. In a few words and without entering into technical details, TQM is based on three cornerstones: quality planning, quality control and quality audit. The third cornerstone means that every economic unit should critically audit its performance, the goods it produces or the service it renders, in order to discover through this critical process what is needed to achieve further progress. In other words, economic success is directly related to the benefits of criticism; a type of criticism which aims at a continuous process of improvement to ensure competitiveness in a market that will have no place or 'mercy' for those who fail to meet the necessary standards

A. Self-criticism

Which aspect of contemporary Egyptian thinking requires a full-scale change? The answer is complacency:

- Any fair-minded outsider cannot deny that Egypt made, throughout the past decade, excellent moves towards a much better economic standard. Nonetheless the inability to admit the gigantic mistakes of the 1950s and 1960s continue to impede the introduction of new systems that would undeniably make the past decade's achievements much greater. It must be said that the way the economy was structured and managed since the mid-1950s was a complete mess. Most of the systems engineered during this era ought to be replaced by systems that proved to be successful in the advanced economies.
- Despite well-deserved pride in Egypt's history, this should not produce complacency but on the contrary an admission that many features of contemporary life ought to be changed in order to once again achieve great results.
- Both the advocates of 'medieval fundamentalism' and equally the old guard of 'the totalitarian era of the 1960s' are the true enemies of the great efforts to build a modern, stable and flourishing Egypt. The first group advocates an illusion that would produce a throwback into the Middle Ages. The second group has led the nation on a long journey of failures; both groups would cut ties with the world in an age when the global system require full participation in all kinds of exchange.

'Self-criticism' undeniably fosters positive, active citizens, members of the society who profoundly believe that they can make a difference. With decreasing complacency and a growing ability to practise self-criticism we shall not disregard conspiracy as a phenomenon, but we shall certainly relate more of our major problems to the way things are/have been managed within our borders. For instance, we shall thence accept that the catastrophic living conditions in too many areas such as the Imbaba district of Cairo are not the result of an imperialist or Israeli plot.

In short, there is no saying more eloquent than that of the great philosopher Emmanuel Kant, that criticism is the most constructive tool ever produced by the human mind.[2]

III. THE FLEXIBILITY OF COMPROMISE

Adding to the absence of critical minds there is doubt about the existence of a distinctive class of intelligentsia in all the Arabic-speaking countries. Ever since the 1950s, most Arab regimes have been careful to create what can only be called 'the official intellectual'. This 'official intellectual' may be an excellent reader and researcher but is almost invariably no more than a civil servant with none of the independence crucial to the creation of a free-thinking, effective intelligentsia that is not subservient to the ruling regime.

It is regrettable that a large number of intellectuals in Arab society have been lured by the petrodollars of the Bedouins who rule the Arabian Peninsula and the Baathists who ruled Syria and Iraq, while others have been prey to the law of attraction to official positions. Thus have most Arab countries unfortunately become devoid of free-thinking intellectuals, and if further proof were needed, it is sufficient to note that almost all intellectuals in the Arab world today churn out identical views on most issues, a phenomenon that is – to put it mildly – uncivilized and uncultured.

Rationality has suffered two major defeats: the first was the triumph of the school which slavishly aped the beliefs and dogmas that developed between the tenth and thirteenth centuries over the school of reason. The end of centuries of relatively enlightened thought paved the way for stagnation, inflexibility and inertia. The second blow was the defeat of the Egyptian school of enlightenment, exemplified by individuals such as Ahmad Lutfi al-Sayyed; Salama Musa (1887–1958), a journalist and reformer with a wide range of interests and an inspiration for Naguib Mahfuz; Taha Husayn; Ali Abd al-Razik, stripped of his al-Azhar degree in 1924 because of his book which opposed rulers of the time; and al-Aqqad, before he retracted his views upon his dismissal from the Wafd party.

Perhaps the last of these great thinkers were Louis Awad (1915–1990); Husayn Fawzi (1900–1988); and Zaki Naguib Mahmud (1905–1993), who was described by al-Aqqad as 'the philosopher of authors and author of philosophers'.

Egypt in the 1920s was undergoing an intellectual boom in its capacity as a leading Mediterranean country. Consider, for example, Fawzi. He graduated with a medical degree from the Egyptian University in 1925 and then travelled to France to study ophthalmology. There, however, he changed his studies to classical music and marine biology. In 1931 he returned to Egypt, where he pursued a scientific research path as professor in the Faculty of Science, advocated Western culture in parallel, and wrote extensively about symphonic music. When Sadat signed the Camp David Treaty with Israel, Fawzi was one of its strongest supporters.[3] Many refer to him as 'Sindbad' due to the fact that he spent three years in the Indian Ocean in the 1930s pursuing marine research.

Today, a new school of enlightenment is beginning to make its presence felt in Egypt and other Arab countries and it will eventually prevail, even if present-day liberals do not witness this outcome during their lifetimes. The battle of progress with reactionary forces can only end in the triumph of the enlightened. Tolerance, criticism (including self-criticism), compromise and diversity are bound to replace hostility, self-praise and apathy.

It is revealing to note, however, that there is no equivalent in the Arabic language – whether classical or colloquial – for the English word 'compromise', which is most commonly translated into Arabic by two words, literally meaning 'halfway solution'. The same is true of several other words such as 'integrity', for which no single word exists in the Arabic language. As language is not merely a tool of communication but also the depositary of a society's cultural heritage, reflecting its way of thinking and the spirit in which it proceeds, as well as the cultural trends which have shaped it, this phenomenon has political, economic and social implications.

Anyone with long experience in dealing with Western institutions would notice that people with a west European background use the word 'compromise' more frequently than those coming from an eastern cultural tradition. Those with an Arab mentality use the word 'compromise' less than those with a Latin mentality, and so too do the latter, using it less frequently than those with an Anglo-Saxon outlook. There is a simple explanation for this. If one's way of thinking is based on a set of philosophical and religious principles, then it is likely that people raised in an Arab culture will be less inclined to use the word compromise than those whose minds were conditioned in a Latin context, where, although the philosophical dimension looms large, the religious perspective figures less prominently than it does in the Arab mentality.

The English philosopher Jeremy Bentham (1748–1832), a major influence on the reforming thought of the nineteenth century, believed that all systems, laws, institutions and ideas should be based on the principle of utility ('utilitarianism'). The United States, for its part, produced two renowned philosophers, William James (1842–1910) and John Dewey (1859–1952),[4] whose works took a broadly parallel stance, though with modifications dictated by the passing of time and unfolding events, advocating what came to be known as 'pragmatism'.

The notion of compromise spread beyond the Anglo-Saxon world into societies belonging to different cultural traditions. In Asia, for example, people of Chinese, Japanese and Indian stock managed, while jealously guarding their cultural specificity, to learn the meaning of the English word 'compromise' before they learned its linguistic form, tending in all their dealings to find solutions based on compromise. Even the Latin countries adopted the notion before the word became part of their political lexicon.

In the Arabic-speaking part of the world, many individuals, even educated people, associate the word 'compromise' with negative terms such as 'submission', 'retreat', 'capitulation', 'weakness' and 'defeat'. These are terms that do not occur to a Westerner when using the word 'compromise' because whatever their educational formation, whether it is in the field of science, humanities or liberal arts, they know that all ideas are in their essence nothing but compromises.

Moreover, the cultures of merchant nations – of which Britain is perhaps the most notable example – have instilled the idea of compromise in all spheres of life, intellectual, political, economic, cultural and social, even in human dealings. Thus, while our popular sayings reflect a negative picture of the term compromise, hundreds of popular sayings in Britain do just the opposite.

Although Islamic scripture is totally compatible with a culture characterized by compromise, Muslim history (especially its Arab chapter) has proceeded in a spirit antithetical to the notion of compromise. Recent history is made up largely of losses which could have been avoided had there not been a persistent rejection of compromise as tantamount to submission, retreat, surrender, capitulation, and even, as some of our more fiery orators put it, as a form of bondage to the will of others.

This 'all-or-nothing' mentality is self-defeating. Any dispute or conflict is, by definition, a struggle between people or nations with different views and at different levels of power. It follows that any resolution of their differences that is not based on a compromise is impossible, because it would entail the total subjugation of the will, interests and power of one of the parties to those of the other. Such a conflict-resolution approach is doomed to fail because it runs counter to the laws of science, nature, and life itself.

Some prominent Egyptian intellectuals like Dr Milad Hanna, an engineer and well-known writer, have tirelessly expounded on the need to accept the 'Other'. Dr Murad Wahba, a philosophy professor and former leftist,[5] has written extensively on the theme that nobody can claim to hold a monopoly on absolute Truth. Such thinkers are making a valuable and noble contribution to the process of instilling the rules and culture of compromise in our society.

The spread of a religious culture based on strict orthodoxy or the textual reading of scripture was one of the reasons for the failure of the concept of compromise to catch on in our culture. If we were to talk to Ibn Rushd or al-Jahez, a renowned Mu'tazalite literary figure, we would find it easy to explain to them, and they would find it easy to grasp the notion, that all thinking, all dealings, must be characterized by a spirit of compromise, with all its implications.

That would not be the case if we spoke with proponents of the orthodox school, strict 'textualists' like Ahmad Ibn Hanbal, Ibn Taymiyya, Ibn Qayyim al-Jawziyya, and Muhammad Ibn Abd al-Wahhab, or with dozens of their contemporary counterparts who preach a dogmatic adherence to the letter rather than the spirit of religion, slamming the doors shut in the face of rationality. Attempting to explain the notion of compromise to members of this school today would be as much of a lost cause as Ibn Rushd's vigorous defence of the primacy of reason eight centuries ago.

Actually, it would be even more of a lost cause because, although

Ibn Rushd was vanquished by the 'textualists' of the Arab/Islamic civilization, his ideas took root in the Christian culture. There is no doubt that the ideas of this great Islamic philosopher prevailed over those of Thomas Aquinas[6] in the thirteenth century thanks to his many disciples in the University of Paris at the time, and the so-called Latin 'Averroists'.[7] Perhaps history will one day admit that an Arab Muslim was behind the victory of reason over dogma at a time when the prevailing culture in Europe was inimical to intellectual initiative and freedom of thought. Had the outcome of the battle for the hearts and minds of the Europeans favoured the other camp, Europe would not have been today at that stage of development and enlightenment.

A similar battle is now underway in our region, a battle of which the outcome is uncertain. If reason is to prevail over obscurantist thinking, immediate action is required. To make a beginning, a team of intellectuals with a cultural formation made up of a synthesis of Arab, Islamic, and other humanistic cultures should come together and lay down a charter to instil the rationale of compromise in the minds of the young people of the Arab countries through educational curricula. This requires promoting the idea that compromise is the strongest product of nature, life and the march of civilizations and cultures, while a rigid refusal to consider the merits of anyone else's opinion and to insist on obtaining all one's demands runs counter to the logic of science, nature, humanity, culture and civilization. It also led to the apathy so apparent everywhere in contemporary Arab society.

NOTES

1. Most of them were annexed to the Ottoman Empire at the beginning of the sixteenth century and remained under the wings of this historic superpower till its defeat in the First World War in 1918.
2. Immanuel Kant, *Selections* (Glasgow: Jackson, Wylie, 1927).
3. Mahmoud Fawzi, *Camp David fi 'aql Wozara' Kharijiat Misr* [Camp David in the Minds of Egypt's Ministers of Foreign Affairs] (Cairo: Madbouli Bookshop, 1990) available at http://www.jamaa.cc/book11702.html.
4. John S. Mill and Jeremy Bentham, *Utilitarianism and Other Essays* (Harmondsworth and New York: Penguin, 1987). William James, *Essays in Pragmatism*, (New York: Hafner, 1948). John Dewey, *Reconstruction in Philosophy* (New York: Henry Colt, 1920).
5. Milad Hanna, *Hewār al Thaqafāt wa Qubuūl al-Ākhar* [The Dialogue Between Cultures and Accepting the Other] (Cairo: Al-iᶜlamiya, 1998). Murad Wahba, *Mullāk Al Haqīqah Al*

Mutlaqa [Beholders of the Absolute Truth] (1998) available at: http://www.4shared.com/get/60456761/c59d98dd/___.html;jsessionid=AE0C5FE61B8D003E15DC2B8A5781E570.dc156.

6. 1225–1274. Italian Catholic priest, proponent of natural theology; he believed that truth can be known through 'reason' and 'faith'.
7. Followers of Averroes (Ibn Rushd).

10

Negativity and Apathy: Consequences of Marginalization

The pattern of behaviour displayed by the victims of poverty differs from one culture to another. In some cultures, it takes the form of a defiant refusal to succumb to the grip of poverty and an openly rebellious expression of that refusal; in others it engenders an attitude of resignation marked by a docile acceptance of what fate has decreed. Many factors determine which of the two patterns will prevail. Societies which have been subjected to tyranny and oppression for much of their history and have a tradition of venerating their rulers will tend to exhibit the second pattern, accepting their lot philosophically and expressing their disillusionment by using the weapon of sarcasm against public officials, but only in private conversations conducted behind closed doors.

In some countries, this mechanism gives rise to political jokes which reflect what people would have wanted to say openly but which, in the absence of available channels, they are forced to express in epigrammatic form. The ability of some of the political jokes thus spawned to encapsulate prevailing opinions and impressions in terse, witty aphorisms is sometimes nothing short of brilliant.

Despots realize only too well that their people's economic independence and the existence of an economically self-sufficient middle class can have disastrous consequences for them. Such economic independence allows a people to move from apathy to action, from a resigned acceptance of whatever the ruler decides at his absolute discretion to active participation in political life. Accountability is the last thing an absolute ruler wants, knowing that his grip on power cannot survive open questions on the source of his legitimacy or on the legitimacy of the privileges he and his cronies enjoy.

I. APATHY, EDUCATION AND TEAMWORK

Modern educational systems in advanced societies are not based on traditional teaching methods in which the teacher is relegated to the role of a transmitter, so to speak, and the student to that of a receiver. Rather they are based on a feedback process involving student participation, dialogue and exchanges of views.

One of the main features of this process is the division of classes into groups which are required to seek answers to given questions for themselves, by accessing available literature on the subject, whether in libraries or on the Internet, by comparing notes and/or consulting together; they finally present the conclusions reached in the light of their research. This sort of group endeavour promotes a team spirit among its members, develops a sense of participation and the conviction that every individual is entitled to seek the truth for himself and to express the truth as they see it openly and fearlessly. It also promotes tolerance and a respect for the right of any member of a group to differ from the majority opinion without this necessarily rupturing the overall cohesion of the group. At the same time, it develops the critical faculties of the students and ensures that they will not elevate anyone to the status of all-knowing oracle, neither teachers, authors nor, by extension, political leaderships.

Students brought up in this system, which recognizes and consecrates the value of teamwork, grow into citizens equipped to participate effectively in the life of their community. By the same token, students brought up under the system of learning by rote, where the relationship between student and teacher is a one-way street, never develop a team spirit, and are content to remain passive recipients of information that will never be translated into active participation in public life. Nor is the material spoon-fed by the teachers processed by the students, who merely learn it by heart and reproduce it word for word in their exam papers, only to forget it afterwards, rather than retain the context or gist.

An educational system which is based on the quantity of material that can be stuffed into young minds rather than on the quality of the values that should go into their formation, which consecrates the cult of personality and fosters blind obedience to diktats from above rather than the spirit of pluralism that is the driving force of progress and civilization, and which does not teach students how to accept criticism and engage in self-criticism can only produce a breed of passive citizens incapable of dealing with life's challenges, as well as participating in the political life of their community. The inflexibility of the system by which they were governed throughout their formative years is capable of killing any initiative. Moreover, the fact that this system denied them the right to choose, which is the essence of political participation, instils in them a spirit of apathy and a sense that any attempt to change the status quo is an exercise in vain.

II. APATHY AND THE RULE OF LAW

Most political systems in the Third World claim to uphold the rule of law, but this is usually an empty boast rather than an accurate reflection of reality. The majority of these systems operate according to the absolute will of an absolute ruler who is answerable to no one for the decisions he makes. More often than not, these decisions serve to encourage the spread of corruption and protect the vested interests of the ruling establishment, in the total absence of either democracy or the rule of law to which these political systems pay continuous lip service. It is not surprising that in such a climate apathy should spread. People are only motivated to participate in public life when it is governed by the rule of law. Conversely, when the decision-making process is clearly designed to serve the interests of a select few at the expense of society as a whole, people accept what they cannot change. There is thus a direct relationship between the absence of the rule of law and the apathy of the citizen.

III. APATHY OF CITIZENS IN AN AUTOCRACY

The discourse of most undemocratic systems of government is rife with reverential references to 'the people'. Following a time-honoured tradition, they glorify the people as an abstract concept, but do not display anywhere near as much respect and concern for its constituent elements, especially the individual citizens. There is a glaring discrepancy between the glorification of the entity known as 'the people' in the official discourse of the state and the abasement of the citizen on a daily basis at the hands of the system, whether in governmental offices, police stations, or hospitals, where no attempt is made to translate the dignity accorded to the people collectively in principle into common courtesy for the individual citizen.

In short, undemocratic systems of government pay lip service to an abstract non-existent entity known as 'the people', while treating citizens much as the Mamluksi treated their Egyptian subjects in one of the darkest chapters of Egypt's history.[1] The tyranny and oppression to which the Egyptians were subjected by a caste of slaves they themselves had bought, and to whom they then inexplicably handed the reins of power, have left traces in Egypt's general cultural climate. The best description of the long shadow cast by nearly three centuries of Mamluk rule on present-day Egypt can be found in a book titled *Turath al-ʿabeed* [The Heritage of Slavery] by an eminent Egyptian author.[2]

IV. APATHY AND THE HERD MENTALITY

Undemocratic systems of government engender a cultural climate which can only be described as a 'herd culture'. Under these systems, the government treats people like cattle, with the result that citizens gradually come to display many of the characteristics of a herd mentality, including a retreat from individualism which, along with democracy, is one of the greatest achievements of human civilization and a prerequisite for the consecration of human rights – in the genuine sense of the term, not in the sense it is bandied about by some of the most despotic systems of government today. Once a herd mentality takes hold of any society, the members of that society will develop a passive attitude incommensurate with the requirements of good citizenship.

A positive attitude that leads citizens to involve themselves in the workings of their society requires a perception of the self as an individual human being, not as an anonymous member of an abstract and dehumanized group known as 'the people'. A useful device for despots, the term 'the people', which is not necessarily the same thing as 'the citizens', allows them to benefit from the apathy and indifference of their subjects. This indifference, one of the main symptoms of a herd culture, is most graphically illustrated in the low turnout at the polls by educated voters who simply could not be bothered to participate in the electoral process.

V. THE 'BIG TALK' SYNDROME

In our tongues so glib,
Our very deaths reside;
We have paid dearly for our gift of the gab.

Nizar Qabbani

No wonder the war ended in defeat, not victory,
For we waged it with all the Orient's gift for oratory,
With quixotic hyperbole that never killed a fly,
Fighting in the logic of fiddle and drum. [3]

Nizar Qabbani

In the 1960s Egypt and the Arabic-speaking world in general claimed to be the stronger military power in the Middle East, a claim that was revealed to be nothing more than an empty boast on the morning of 5 June 1967. To the same extent that we overrated our own abilities, we underestimated those of what was called 'our historical enemy', which was dismissed as 'a bunch of Jewish gangs'. Events were to prove that the enemy was far more dangerous than we had talked ourselves into believing. Nor were these the only instances of 'big-talk' during the 1960s, a decade that has become synonymous with hyperbole. A number of other notorious examples come to mind: the description of the British prime minister as an 'effete sissy', a particularly offensive characterization in the Arabic language; the taunting of the United States of America by inviting its president to 'go drink from the sea, first from the Red Sea and, when it dries up, from the Mediterranean'; the boasting of the Egyptian Qahar (Conqueror) and Zafar (Victorious) missiles as the ultimate weapon that was going to remove Israel from the face of the earth. My father used to mock these huge missiles (when they were paraded) by saying 'an excellent carpenter has done a very good job', that they were not real missiles but huge maquettes (wooden models). His statement reflected the views of the pre-1952 Egyptian revolution generation on the socialist era of Nasser.

When we listen to the rousing national songs composed in the 1960s, we find that, despite their high artistic standard and beauty of the national and pan-Arab dream they celebrated, their lyrics are replete with big-talk. The tendency to indulge in bombastic and high-flown language continued and grew throughout the 1970s, 1980s and 1990s. Now it is such an integral part of our public life that anyone using a different language today strikes a discordant note.

Thus when we talk of our history, we do not use scientific and objective language; we invariably sink into grandiloquent rhetoric that drowns the truth in a welter of words. The same pattern applies to our approach to the 'here and now'. Even something as simple as a victory by the national football team provides an excuse for a veritable word fest. Although at the international level our standard in the game ranks somewhere between 'average' and 'poor', on the rare occasions our players score a victory on the football field – as happened at the 2006 Africa Cup championship – we are not in the least embarrassed to hail them as 'conquering Pharaohs' or to use similarly overblown language to describe what is, after all, nothing more than the outcome of a match.

The use of superlatives is rampant in our media where, as a look at the front page of any newspaper will show, big-talk is the order of the day. Thus any meeting is a 'summit' meeting; any decision a 'historic' decision.

It must be said in all fairness that our propensity to use big-talk is in no way contrived: we are only doing what comes naturally. High-flown language has become part and parcel of our code of communication, both oral and written. It is not associated in our minds with obsequiousness or fawning; we do not use it in order to curry favour or to ingratiate ourselves with the object of our flattery, but we use it as a spontaneous form of expression. Sadly, this reflects a serious flaw in our mental construction that has become deeply entrenched in our culture. Even the few who are conscious of the problem are themselves not above succumbing to the big-talk syndrome on occasion, proving that the problem has pervaded our cultural climate to the point where no one is immune against its effects.

An example that graphically illustrates how this feature has come to dominate the cultural landscape in the area is the Egyptian television coverage of the marathon that took place around the pyramids shortly after the Luxor massacre – when jihadists killed, wounded and in some case mutilated 100 foreign tourists – in the autumn of 1997. Viewers were treated to the amazing spectacle of about ten foreigners – interviewed separately and supposedly at random – who all said the same thing in virtually the same words, as though reading from a prepared script: 'Egypt is a safe country in which we feel secure … Terrorism does not exist only in Egypt but in all parts of the world … Everyone wants to visit Egypt and see its wonderful antiquities.' This feature is unique to this culture, a mark of dubious distinction that sets us apart from other members of the community of nations, whether Western or Eastern.

Cultural evolution in the countries belonging to Western civilization, including North America, has proceeded along a course that equates 'big talk' with ignorance. Human knowledge is a complex web of interconnected strands in which there is no room for big-talk, but only for moderate, sensible and unpretentious language that tries as far as possible to reflect the unembellished realities of science and culture. As for Eastern civilizations, the reserve that has always been – and continues to be – one of their most prominent characteristics shields them from any temptation to indulge in big-talk.

The picture is very different in Arab societies, where the temptation is indulged to the utmost. Indeed, the big-talk syndrome is endemic to our culture, which has a long tradition of declamatory rhetoric that places more value on the beauty of the words used than on their accurate reflection of reality. Nowhere is this more evident than in the rich body of Arabic poetry, which is full of poems eulogizing or vilifying this or that ruler, for reasons known only to the poet and often having nothing to do with reality.

The dichotomy between language and truth is not only acceptable in our culture, but it is actually honoured in a famous saying: 'the most beautiful poetry is the least truthful' (*a'thab al she'r ... akthabu*). The issue is addressed by no less authoritative a source than the Quran itself, when it denounces poets as 'drifters in all directions', and of not practising what they preach (*Surat al-Shu'ara* (Poets), *Sura* 26:224).

The writer of these lines believes it is incumbent on all those who are aware of this distortion in the Arab mentality to raise national awareness of the dangers inherent in using big-talk that is totally divorced from reality. To that end, they must expose the negative effects of a phenomenon which has led some to describe us a 'culture of words' or, with scientific progress, 'of microphones'.

Educational curricula must be designed to alert our youth to the highly detrimental effects of this phenomenon, which not only distorts our image in the eyes of the outside world but also keeps us imprisoned in a fantasy world that we have created for ourselves with no basis in reality. It also holds us hostage to a past we evoke in such glowing terms that it becomes more attractive than any present. There is no doubt that the big-talk syndrome is linked to a number of other negative features, such as lack of objectivity, escaping into the past, excessive self-praise and inability to accept criticism. Indeed, it would be no exaggeration to say that it is the bridge that links all these negative features together.

It is also important to emphasize the link between the big-talk syndrome and the narrow margin of democracy. In a cultural climate dominated by hyperbole, it is as difficult to expand the margin of democracy as it is easy for political forces to win adherents through the use of demagogy. Those who claim that their political project represents 'the solution' to all the ills of the Arab societies are merely serving up another course in an interminable and indigestible meal of big-talk. Economic and social problems today are far too complex to be cured by simple slogans rooted in the big-talk syndrome.

The words of Nizar Qabbani eloquently sum up the situation in these words:

> *We have donned a thin veneer of civilization*
> *While our souls remain mired in the Dark Ages.*[4]

Sheer ignorance and unjustified conceit have led most Arabs to believe in the possibility of creating their own game, played according to rules that differ from those developed by the democratic world. It is the same ignorance that leads some to believe that abiding by the global rules of the game constitutes humiliation or defeat; a sick reasoning spewed forth by those akin to the poets of the pre-Islamic era, where resonant words and grandiose phrases were much admired and indeed constituted the only achievement of this age.

NOTES

1. Members of a former military caste originally composed of slaves from Turkey, which held the Egyptian throne from about 1250 until 1517 and remained powerful until 1811.
2. ᶜA. ᶜA., *Turath Al-ᶜabeed* [The Heritage of Slavery] (Cairo: Al Maktab Al ᶜarabi Lel Maāref, 1998).The author of the book (A.A.) wrote an introduction which made him unable to put his name on the cover of the book; it would (according to him) have caused his murder in a society that has a very thin layer of tolerance to criticism. However A.A. was a professor of sociology at one of the Egyptian universities and advocated the theory that most Egyptians are similar (from a sociological viewpoint) to African-Americans in the United States, in that the latter suffered from the harsh treatment as secondary citizens United States and the former from non-Egyptian rulers of Egypt for some twenty centuries – since the end of the last Ancient Egyptian dynasty in the fourth century BC.
3. Author's translation from Arabic.
4. Nizar Qabbani, *Hawamwsh ala daftar al naksa* [Margins on the Notes of Defeat] (1967), available at http://www.damascus-online.com/poems/Nizar/naksah.htm.

11

The 'Self-Praise' Syndrome

The wise man's mind will even in bliss cause him misery,
While the fool in abject misery will a happy man be.
It is vain to separate from his ignorance,
He who does not repent;
Or to address him, he who lacks sagacity.[1]

Al-Mutanabbi (915–965)

Another defect of the Arab mentality which has come to manifest itself conspicuously in the discourse is the tendency to indulge in excessive self-praise. This defect has spawned aberrant social values in everyday lives. Nowhere is this tendency to sing our own praises more evident than in the mass media which, day in, day out, feed our self-infatuation by tirelessly extolling our virtues and glorifying our achievements. The same pattern is repeated at the individual level, where boastfulness and self-promotion are fast becoming the norm.

This has not always been the case, when the mass media today is compared with the newspapers and magazines that appeared in Egypt half a century ago. Also, the comparison of the mass media in the Arabic-speaking world with those in other parts of the world, especially the developed countries, shows the latter is unique when it comes to an overweening sense of self-satisfaction expressed in a constant torrent of self-praise.

The phenomenon only began to appear, in a diffident sort of way, some twenty-five years ago, reaching its present brazen proportions in the last twenty years, with a noticeable leap in the last decade. It is virtually impossible to read a newspaper or magazine today without coming across one or more articles and/or news items lauding our achievements, superiority and virtues. Often these paeans of praise are attributed to a foreign source, as though this imbues them with greater value.

Although much of the material published in this respect inspires more incredulity than credibility, the phenomenon shows no signs of abating but rather continues to indulge an apparently insatiable need for self-aggrandizement by loudly and incessantly proclaiming how wonderful we are.

For example, not a day goes by without one of the following or similar statements appearing in Egyptian papers:

- The international community praises Egypt's economic reforms.
- The World Bank praises the Egyptian model of economic development.
- According to this or that university, the Egyptian economy is strong and stands on solid grounds.
- According to such and such a centre for economic studies, the Egyptian economy will never be exposed to an economic crisis like the one that shook the Asian tigers.
- UNESCO decides to implement the Egyptian experiment in this or that area at the global level.

What does this mean? And why do we not read similar statements in any French, German, English, Japanese or American newspaper? How can our constant harping on the same theme be explained? To my mind, the explanation lies in a desire to escape from a harsh reality into a fantasy world we have created to fulfil a psychological need for a reality more to our liking. Escapism is by definition a negative reaction, a passive acceptance of the status quo and a tacit admission of inability to change it.

The only way we can change the status quo and overcome our many problems is to adopt a more positive and constructive approach to the reality in which we are living. This entails admitting that we are beset by huge economic and social problems; that we are, unfortunately (and it must be said, unnecessarily), a Third World country, and that these problems are a direct result of the way public life in Egypt was administered in the century and a half since the death of Mohamed Ali in 1849.

It is only when we abandon the pattern of excessive self-praise which we all know to be empty of any real substance and start admitting and facing up to our problems that we can begin to achieve progress at all levels.

Of course, stemming the torrent of self-praise which is drowning this society and diverting it into constructive self-criticism is far from being an easy undertaking. Its success depends on our ability to sow the seeds of positive values in young minds through educational curricula. But these will only yield fruit in the long term. In the short term, a start must be made from the top of the pyramid, not its base. Once we admit to ourselves how bad the situation really is, the next logical step is to ask why such a sorry state of affairs is occurring.

The answer lies in the ineptitude of some of the leaderships in the middle of the previous century. It is important to emphasize that evaluating the performance of public officials in today's world is not based on their adoption of specific ideologies. Efficient administration depends, rather, on the availability of an executive cadre at the summit of society, with a pragmatic approach to problem-solving, more concerned with implementing the results of experiments that proved to be successful, than in getting bogged down in futile and vain ideological debates that only hamper progress and perpetuate the status quo.

I. THE 'STAYING-PUT' SYNDROME

Friends!
What is poetry if it does not declare mutiny?
If it does not topple tyrants?
What is poetry if it does not stir up volcanoes where we need them?
What is poetry if we cannot dislodge the crown
Worn by the powerful kings of this world?[2]

Nizar Qabbani

For a person to want to remain in a privileged position is a perfectly normal human instinct. But when the instinct turns into an obsession, it becomes a cultural phenomenon with political, economic, social and psychological implications. Over the last twenty-five years, the desire of people in high places to cling to their positions has grown exponentially, to a degree never witnessed before in Egypt or, for that matter, in any society that enjoys political and social mobility, in societies marked with a high degree of democracy.

This is not how successful international corporations work. Instead they follow guiding principles which they uphold strictly and unconditionally:

- The cultural premise that the driving engine of success is the institution itself and not any individual.
- A policy that abjures the notion that rewarding an individual for

exceptional performance is by retaining that person in the same position indefinitely. For the well-being of the institution itself and in terms of sound management, the belief that no single individual is indispensable – and hence irreplaceable – makes more sense than the idea that a person who performs his/her job well and achieves good results has acquired the right to a lifelong tenure of the position. Thus, many corporations have adopted the following policies:

- Occupancy of an executive position must not exceed a period of three to five years.
- Any person who reaches the age of retirement must retire, no matter how exceptionally brilliant, competent and talented he/she may be.

Conversely, a culture of 'staying put' has pervaded Egypt in the last quarter of a century. Anyone occupying the top position in any given area – the president of a club, for example, or of a professional syndicate or a political party – considers the position a lifelong sinecure. The word 'former' when applied to a minister not reappointed in a cabinet reshuffle is tantamount to referring to him or her as the 'late' so and so. Departure from a high position sets the rumour mills rolling: the occupant has either fallen foul of the powers that be, or performance was so poor that the official had to be removed.

More than a quarter of a century ago, François Mitterrand, then the president of France, called on President Anwar Sadat. As he was leaving, he told Sadat that he would be going on to visit Muhammad Hasanayn Haykal, the leading Egyptian journalist. The Egyptian president's immediate reaction to this bit of news was to exclaim: 'But I fired him!' President Mitterrand told friends later that he could not understand what that had to do with his decision to meet with Haykal: 'I didn't say I was going to call on the editor of *al-Ahram* (newspaper);[3] I said I was going to call on Muhammad Hasanayn Haykal.'

When the story was related to me by Mitterrand's daughter, I said that her father's inability to understand Sadat's remark was due to the different cultural backgrounds and mentalities of the two men. For Sadat, as for many of our countrymen, a person's worth is measured in terms of the position he holds and the titles that precede his name. Thus if Haykal's value stemmed from his position as editor-in-chief of *al-Ahram*, then it follows that when Sadat fired him, he became a worthless nobody – hence Sadat's surprise that Mitterrand would want to meet him nevertheless.

Nothing, of course, could be further from the truth. Although I differ with Mr Haykal on most political issues, he is far and away the best journalist in the Arabic-speaking world. I was lunching with him at a restaurant in London a few years ago when he called the Spanish royal palace to request an appointment with King Juan Carlos two days later. After only fifteen minutes, the palace called him back to confirm that the king would be happy to see him. This is a man whose books have been translated into many languages and read by millions of people throughout the world. His critics vilify him to ingratiate themselves with their benefactors. Not a single one of them is capable of putting together a manuscript that would be acceptable to any international publisher.

This kind of attitude that associates personal status absolutely with social position almost certainly is what led the university professor and former dean of the Faculty of Law to enter into a pitched battle with his rivals using live ammunition, in a bid to stay on as president of an opposition party against the will of its members. Perhaps he would not have been so determined to cling to his position at the head of the party if he had remembered that its founder, who held no official position, was more popular than both Egypt's king and its prime minister. Similarly violent battles were fought over the presidency of a famous sports club. These and hundreds of other examples show how far people will go to cling to their privileged positions; nobody today accepts the idea that occupancy of these positions is temporary and not a permanent state of affairs.

A book was recently published about the monarchs who ruled Egypt over thousands of years,[4] beginning with the founder of the First Dynasty in 3400 BC, the Pharaoh Menes who unified Upper and Lower Egypt. A simple statistical survey shows that these rulers can be divided into three numerically equal groups:

1. Those who were forcibly removed from the throne.
2. Those who died in office.
3. Those who were killed in office.

Not a single ruler can be found who voluntarily abdicated. But there is one partial exception. On Wednesday 8 October 1917, the ruler of Egypt, Sultan Husayn Kamal, died. In accordance with the rules of succession, the throne was offered to his son, Prince Kamal al-Din

Husayn, who turned down the offer. The throne went instead to the 'blackguard' prince, the sultan's younger brother, Ahmad Fu'ad. No one remembers Kamal al-Din's name. The explanation for this collective amnesia is that in Egypt's culture, anyone who actually turns down the chance to wield absolute power must be demented and hence not worth remembering. And so, a man of high principle, an idealist who exercised his free will in the face of the ultimate temptation, has been relegated to oblivion.

The word 'blackguard' to describe Prince Ahmad Fu'ad came from the poet Bayram al-Tunsi who lamented the accession of a prince best known for his love of cabarets, which exceeds his regard for his own throne. His famous poem goes:

When in Egypt we ran out of kings,
The British brought you and threw you in the ring,
They sat you on the throne to masquerade as a king true,
Where did they find a traitor and blackguard like you?[5]

NOTES

1. Author's translation from Arabic.
2. Author's translation from Arabic.
3. The most widely read Egyptian daily newspaper, founded in 1875.
4. Nasser Al Ansary, *Mawsu'at Hukkām Misr min al fara'ena ila al yawm* [Encyclopedia of the Rulers of Egypt from the Pharaohs till Today] (Cairo: Shorouk, 1994).
5. Bairam Al-Tunsi, *Mujrim wa dun* [Criminal and Low], available at http://www.elm7ata.org/vb/showthread.php?t=8723. Author's translation from Arabic.

12

Destructive Beliefs

Those who accede to the 'throne' cling to their positions and remain there eternally, and the vicious circle continues: abuse of big-talk and self-praise, denial of misconceptions and what it entails of false beliefs covering over our weaknesses and inadequacies.

I. COMPLACENCY

A. The Other Face of the Denial Culture

There can be no process of constructive criticism of our mistakes and shortcomings before overcoming the insistence on denying their existence – through denial or ignoring them – in the first place.

The road to progress should proceed in three stages. The first is to break out of the denial mentality. The second is to embark on a process of constructive criticism while avoiding personalizing the process by using it as an opportunity to vilify certain individuals. The fact is that no one in the region is entirely blameless for the predicament, and finger-pointing will help no one. The third stage is to come up with concrete proposals on how to best solve problems. There can be no shortcuts here, no way of jumping directly to the third stage before first, breaking out of our denial mentality, and second, embarking on a process of constructive criticism of all misconceptions and shortcomings once it is admitted that these do exist.

During my twenty years as a member of the first echelon of a well-known multinational conglomerate in western Europe, East Asia and North America, I was taught that the presence of too many ideology-driven individuals in any society will invariably impede on its going through the necessary stages of the road to progress. There is not a single advanced society on the face of the earth today whose leading and ruling elite is ideology driven. Finding solutions to the complex problems of contemporary life entails using a scientific approach based on empirical verification, and adopting practical solutions that were tested and successfully applied by others, and not on doctrinal formulas dreamt up by ideologists to fit their rigid worldview.

In fact there is a 'prescription' for progress, a mix of values, systems and policies drawn from successful experiments, not from theoretical ideas. The ingredients making up the prescription are the end product of the collective human experience, the cumulative legacy of all the different civilizations that propelled humanity forward over the ages. They belong to the whole of humanity, to the march of human civilization in general, rather than to any specific model of civilization.

One ingredient the prescription for progress does not include is ideology. Indeed, once an ideological mentality takes hold of the opinion-makers of any society, that society's prospects of making any headway on the road to progress are severely diminished. By definition, ideologies are driven by moral certainty in a system of belief, a certainty that can only be sustained by suspending the critical faculties of those adhering to the ideology and building up a defence mechanism against any challenge to their core beliefs. They tend to take refuge in a bunker mentality which leaves little room for self-criticism and even less for breaking down the wall of denial isolating them from reality. Such criticism as they engage in is reserved to being directed at others; yet when it comes to evaluating their own performance, there is nothing but self-praise.

Sceptics could argue that moving from a culture of denial to one in which people are conditioned to accept criticism and to engage in self-criticism requires a lengthy educational process extending over centuries. This argument is easily refuted by evidence to the contrary. In the last forty years, eight developed Asian countries succeeded in overcoming the culture of denial, and adopting a culture that accepts criticism. Indeed, in the cases of South Korea and Malaysia, the process took only twenty years.

Countless books, studies and research papers published all over the world, not only in countries the Arabs once described as enemies (like Britain and the United States) but also in many they call their friends (such as Russia, India, China, Japan and France) have praised Anwar Sadat's foresight, wisdom and political acumen in adopting the line he did towards the Arab-Israeli conflict, especially in the last four years of his life. By the same token they find that the Arab countries, leaderships and intellectuals who fiercely opposed his line at the time committed a grave strategic mistake.

Not content with their virulent campaign of defamation against the late Egyptian president, Arab leaders met in Baghdad in 1978 (the historical irony of that location is clear) to announce their boycott of Sadat and Egypt. One of the victims of their relentless war of words against Sadat was Egypt's former cultural minister, Yusuf al-Seba'i, who was murdered in 1979 while on a visit to Cyprus for no other reason than that he had accompanied the Egyptian president on his visit to Jerusalem two years earlier.

The situation is very different today. Many of those who participated in the anti-Sadat campaign at the time are now trying to follow in his footsteps, albeit far less effectively. Most of his former detractors admit today that they were mistaken not to support him, with no less virulent a critic of his line at the time than the Saudi monarch's brother, who said in 1977 that he wished it was in his power to shoot down the plane carrying Sadat to Jerusalem. Thirty years later the very same prince issued a statement admitting that Sadat was right, and that those who opposed him were wrong. Despite all this, most of us are still unable – or unwilling – to venture beyond the wall of denial behind which we have cloistered ourselves for so long, and, consequently, to recognize a simple truth that is staring us in the face: Sadat was right, his detractors were wrong.

This rigid denial of reality can be motivated only ideologically (whether by pan-Arabism, Nasserism, socialism or by the ideology of the Muslim Brothers). The denial mechanism is brought into play just as strongly with respect to two defining moments in the history of the Arab-Israeli conflict; although everyone would be more than happy today to accept the partition plan offered by the United Nations in 1947,[1] the solid wall of denial we have built to shield ourselves from painful truths prevents us from openly admitting that we committed a strategic mistake in rejecting the plan.

Similarly if we succeed today in restoring the Golan Heights[2] in their entirety to Syria, in ending Israel's occupation of the West Bank, and in restoring East Jerusalem, it would only be restitution of losses incurred in May and June of 1967. Of the territory lost in the 1967 war, only Egypt has managed to recover Sinai. Even those who claim that Egypt was tricked into entering a dark tunnel begun in May and ended on 7 June 1967 must admit that one of the primary responsibilities of any leadership is not to allow anyone to lead it into a trap. But our culture of denial prevents us from looking these facts in the face.

All the books and articles that have been written, all the lectures delivered and all the television and radio programmes broadcast since then avoid touching on these uncomfortable truths. Thus while foreign analysts are unanimous in qualifying our performance on all these occasions of Arab-Israeli wars – 1948, 1949, 1956 and 1967 – as lamentable, we continue to turn a deaf ear, or as the Egyptian saying goes, have 'an ear of mud and an ear of clay' to the truth.

Although Egypt ranks number 123 in the UNDP Human Development Report for 2003,[3] its media have highlighted the few points in the country's favour while totally ignoring the overall picture, which was described by the prominent economist Hazem Al-Beblawy as being 'nothing to be proud of'. But the media, true to form, have been tireless in their attempts to paint a rosy picture of what is actually an indictment of economic performance, with all the major newspapers carrying banner headlines highlighting the one positive point made by the report, and ignoring the many negative points. This is yet another manifestation of the pervasive culture of denial marking every aspect of life.

Denial also serves us well when it comes to the issue of corruption. Of course, corruption has become so rampant in our society that we can no longer actually deny its existence. Instead, we deny its significance, playing down the urgency of the problem by convincing ourselves that corruption is a universal phenomenon, and that it exists in all societies. While this is certainly true, it is also true that the extent, degree and spread of corruption differ from one society to the other. A society in which corruption has become a way of life cannot be compared to those in which isolated cases of corruption are dealt with as aberrations. The same is true of crime; while human nature is the same everywhere, some societies have low rates of crime, others have moderate rates and still others have high rates. A complacent attitude toward the issue of corruption is yet another example of how adept is the denial mechanism in shielding from unpleasant truths.

Admittedly there is a serious management problem and there are complaints about the absence of modern management systems and techniques in Egypt, whether in economic institutions, government departments or service sectors. But like a doctor who proclaims a patient ill without identifying the cause of his disease, the blame is not placed where it belongs: on the role of the state in general and on the executive authority in particular. Little has changed from the days when Egypt was a socialist country following a command economy and little room was left for the development of effective management systems. However, on this all-important issue, the culture of denial rules.

It is common knowledge that Egypt's educational system produces graduates totally unfit to compete on the international job market. They are unfamiliar with the concept of teamwork, their English-language skills are practically non-existent and they are formed by an educational philosophy based on rote learning which actively discourages personal initiative and creativity. Moreover, they are raised to believe that there exists only one model of pure, absolute Truth, with the result that there is very little room in their intellectual baggage for pluralism, dialogue, acceptance of the 'Other' or tolerance.

Another feature shared by the vast majority of graduates churned out by the system is an inability to express their ideas in writing or to conduct methodical research in a scientific manner. But here too is the pattern of denial, patting people on the back for 'achievements' in the field of education while turning a blind eye to serious structural misconceptions in the educational system which lead most international organizations in advanced countries to turn down systematically job applicants who received their education in Arab countries.

The list of examples is endless. The inability to come to grips with so many serious questions is a direct result of the pervasive culture of denial keeping to a closed loop and preventing progress.

II. BELIEF IN CONSPIRACY

Being thorough believers that they are absolutely correct, the Arabs perceive those who do not comply with their beliefs to be enemies who conspire to destroy them. The conspiracy theory is tremendously powerful in Arab societies, including Egypt. There are many who subscribe wholeheartedly to such theories, firmly convinced that sinister forces are busy hatching plots against them. United in their belief, they differ only as to the motives and origins of the conspirators. Some see them as motivated by an atavistic hatred for Muslims in general and Arabs in particular, others by a fear that an Arab awakening represents a danger that must be averted at any cost. Then there are those who attribute the conspiracy to Jewish machinations. Finally there are those who believe it is part of a grand design for the economic exploitation of the region. Actually, in the minds of many millions of Egyptians and Arabs, the following propositions have become virtual articles of faith:

- The blueprint for their recent history and present reality was drawn up by the great powers, and what they are now living through is the product of these machinations.
- The powers responsible for this grand design were Britain and France in the past and the United States, aided and abetted by its protégé, Israel, in the recent past and present.
- The plans were prepared in great detail by those powers, leaving little room for manoeuvre to those at the receiving end who had no choice but to follow the course charted for them.
- Accordingly Arabs bear little responsibility for what happened in the past, what is happening in the present, and indeed, according to some, what will happen in the future. Reality is the predetermined result of a grand design, and it is beyond our power to change it.

When Israel, as an actor, is factored into this theoretical scenario, the picture becomes even more inflammatory and provocative. Moving from generalities to specifics, it is normal from this perspective to see even the landmark events of our modern history as results of the plots hatched by the great powers. These include the 1956 war, Syria's secession from its merger with Egypt in 1961, the Yemen war of 1962, the June 1967 disaster, and the failure to crown the glorious crossing of the Suez Canal in October 1973 with the military liberation of the whole of Sinai, as well as President Sadat's visit to Jerusalem in 1977, the Camp David accords signed between Egypt and Israel, the demise of the Soviet Union, and the structural collapse of socialism everywhere, as well as a large variety of other international events, including economic issues.

The conspiracy theory is shared to varying degrees by these following disparate groups. However, the reasons for their adherence to this theory derive from different sources. First all those who can be classified as 'Islamic' believe profoundly in the truth of the propositions which collectively form the 'conspiracy theory'. The groups in question include the Muslim Brothers, al-Gama'at al-Islamiyya, al-Jihad and all fundamentalist movements, indeed, even the most moderate of these trends. The most devoted adherents of the conspiracy theory are the 'Islamists'.

The Islamists, in all their subdivisions, consider that the history of the region is the history of a conflict between Islam on the one side and the Judeo-Christian world on the other. As far as they are concerned, the Crusades[4] have never stopped, except that now they are not being waged openly on the battlefield but elsewhere. This group attaches great importance to the Jewish dimension, which it blames for many of the ills besetting the Arab/Islamic world and the disasters which have befallen it.

Second all those who can be classified in one way or another under the banner of socialism, from Marxists to socialists, passing through tens of subdivisions of leftist or socialist orientation, including the Nasserites, also subscribe to the conspiracy theory, albeit less rigidly than the Islamists. For while they believe in the theory as a whole and in the propositions on which it is based, their belief is neither shrouded in what can be called the spirit of *jihad* or militancy, nor grounded in anti-Christian feelings as is the case with the 'Islamists'.

The socialist group, in the broad sense of the term, views matters from the perspective of the struggle between what it calls the forces of imperialism, and the oppressed and exploited peoples of the world. Of course the difference in the degree of rigidity of the belief and the fervour of the conviction is due to the theocratic ethos of the Islamic groups and the more scientific, progressive and modern spirit of socialist ideas, even if the failure of those ideas to achieve their aims or live up to their slogans proves that they are inherently flawed.

The third and final group is made up of ordinary citizens in the Arab societies and Egypt, who belong neither to the Islamic school politically nor to the socialist school ideologically; most of these people are inclined to believe in the conspiracy theory and to accept the validity of the propositions on which it rests without questioning it.

This third group, the multitude of ordinary citizens who subscribe to the conspiracy theory, reflects the climate of opinion created by the media, many of the key constituents of which are controlled in this part of the world either by the socialists or by the Islamists, and who repeatedly spout the propositions on which the conspiracy theory rests as if they were gospel. In societies not characterized by a high level of education and culture, the media (including the *minbar* or pulpit of the mosque) can be used to brainwash and indoctrinate public opinion. It is enough to recall that the Ministry of Information[5] in some countries was once called the 'Ministry of Guidance', a clear admission of its intended function: to guide and direct.

Actually the sources from which the three groups draw their belief in the conspiracy theory are wholly illusory, having no basis in fact, history or logic. The history of the peoples of the region would have been the same, including their subjugation by Western colonialism, even if the region had been part of the Christian world. The West did not colonize people because they were Muslims but for quite different reasons. On the one hand, the populations were backward and hence susceptible to foreign domination; easy pickings, as it were. On the other, the whole colonial enterprise was motivated in the first instance by economic considerations, and, to a lesser degree, by cultural or 'civilizational' considerations, which constitute a broader framework than religious factors.

Although much can be said to refute the naïve view that the region's history with Western colonialism can be reduced to a question of religion, it is sufficient here to cite but a few of the many examples attesting the contrary to realize how widely off the mark this view is. Those who maintain there would have been no colonies had it not been for the Muslim heritage forget the dark chapter of history under the dominion of the Ottoman empire, when the colonized Arab peoples were subjected to the worst kinds of abuse by their colonial masters, despite the fact that both colonizer and colonized belonged to the same Muslim faith. Throughout the eighteenth century, there was a deplorable state of backwardness, even though they were Muslims occupied by Muslims, as the Christian West was then still absent from the scene. The same situation prevailed when the Zionist movement was launched by the end of the nineteenth century.[6] Indeed, a state of medieval backwardness persisted for more than six centuries preceding the emergence of the Jews as a political force capable of affecting the course of events in any way.

Though in many ways wrong, the socialist reading of history with the colonial period is right in that it approaches the issue from an economic perspective. The economic factor was the driving force behind the West's imperialist ambitions in the region over the last two centuries. But this was within a framework quite different from that of the conspiracy theory.

As to the group of ordinary citizens enamoured of the conspiracy theory, it is in a way understandable that their logic is impaired and cannot stand up to any sort of serious discussion or analysis; for even the most outlandish statement, if repeated often enough, can come to be accepted as true, especially in a society where half of the population is illiterate, and the other half displays only a very modest standard of education and culture. Here, the lack of sophistication provides a fertile breeding ground for the most untenable, demagogical and unfounded assertions to take root and flourish.

The real issue is that most of those who subscribe to the conspiracy theory know very little about the nature and mechanisms of the capitalist economy or what is called a market or free economy. The essence of capitalism is competition, a notion which means many things, some positive and wholesome, others negative and unhealthy. On the positive side, it works to the benefit of individuals and the enhancement of their quality of life because, by definition, it leads to a process of constant upgrading of the type and quality of products and services; this in turn often leads to reducing their cost or price.

But given that all the ideological alternatives to the market economy have failed lamentably, wreaking such havoc in the societies which adopted them that they have been relegated to the museum of obsolete ideas, we must under no circumstances let our nostalgia for the past or our emotional reaction to certain aspects of capitalism drive us back into the world of socialist ideas. Those ideas have caused so much more loss, damage, and human suffering that they have forfeited the right to be given a second chance. Indeed, experience has proven that socialism (both as an ideology and in terms of practical application) is not a viable system of beliefs.

On the negative side, the free market sometimes deteriorates into vicious struggles between the producers of products and services, struggles that can take such diverse forms as driving a rival out of the market, marginalizing the role of others, and grabbing the largest share of the market or markets. This feature of the Western capitalist system engenders, in countries without a long tradition of industrialization and advanced capitalist services, the belief that they are the victims of a well-planned conspiracy.

Unless this aspect of competition is well understood and accepted as an inevitable – if unfortunate – feature of the market economy, and unless a strategy is devised to deal with it as a fact of life in the contemporary world, no goals will be attained. The competition being referred to here, which is one of the main cornerstones of economic life based on the dynamics of a market economy, was responsible for the wars that tore Europe apart in the last three centuries, indeed, for the two world wars the twentieth century has witnessed.

But after centuries of fighting among themselves, the Europeans came to realize in the last three decades that the advantages of putting an end to the strife that had convulsed their continent throughout much of its history greatly outweighed the advantages of allowing a spirit of contentious competition to continue ruling their lives. And so, competition in its extreme form was displaced from Europe to other arenas. The rationale now governing competition in Europe, which continues to thrive in many different shapes and forms, is mutual coexistence, and consensus on a framework of checks and balances in which competition is to operate.

To better illustrate the point, note a very simple fact, which is that, in an economic system based on competition, the strategic interest of the producer, or seller, is to remain a seller while ensuring that the buyer of his products or services remains a buyer as long as possible, preferably forever. There can be no switching of roles here. This simple principle is the essence of that aspect of competition which many in our part of the world tend to regard as indicative of a conspiracy. Although in a way it does resemble a conspiracy, it is very different in terms of motivation and the rules which determine its inner workings. This law, one of the laws governing competition in a free-market economy, operates within advanced industrial societies. Its application outside those societies is thus inevitable, expected and unavoidable.

In other words, the economic system in force in the advanced industrial countries (now also advanced technologically and in the services sector) is based on unavoidable conflicts fuelled by competition, which manifest themselves in endless attempts to capture the largest possible share of the market. This means that the big fish are constantly trying to swallow the little fish. This process and its negative, not to say ferocious, aspects, operate both inside a given society, and beyond (where it is liable to be even more ferocious).

The terminology and practices of modern management sciences contain many terms and notions that, in the final analysis, serve competition in its various aspects (both positive and negative). Some of these principal notions which have become part of the lexicon of modern management sciences in the contemporary world include quality management, global marketing, data confidentiality, the plethora of occupational health systems and environmental considerations. These and tens of other recently coined terms are tailored essentially to serve the interests of the big fish who, by applying them, can successfully swallow the small fish.

We can now add to the 'big-fish-eat-small-fish' law, another rule running parallel to it, which is that the swift and efficient fish will gobble up the fish that are less swift and efficient. The huge conglomerates that have emerged on the global stage in the last twenty years in the fields of industry, services, technology and commerce attest to the growing ascendancy of this new law. It is very important here to distinguish between what we *want* to see, and what we cannot avoid seeing if we do not want to delude ourselves. These laws/rules exist and are fully operational, and there is no hope, after the demise of socialism, to replace them with laws/rules that can ensure success, abundance and the avoidance of these aberrations (for those who regard them as such).

It must be said that even the most widely read and highly cultured intellectual would be unable to fully grasp those new realities and laws if his cultural formation is based exclusively on a familiarity – no matter how deep and extensive – with human and social sciences, but without any knowledge of the modern sciences in the fields of management, marketing and human resources, and the new specialized fields which have branched out of them. No matter how deeply a person may have drunk from the tree of knowledge, how familiar he is with the works of thinkers from Socrates to Bertrand Russell, passing though the thousands of names and areas of human knowledge, if his cultural baggage does not include a working knowledge of contemporary sciences in the fields of management, marketing and human resources, he will be unable to grasp the essence of these laws. In a way, he would be like a physicist who devotes fifty years of his life studying physics since the dawn of history with the exception of the last half century. Although in such a case he would be well acquainted with the history of the subject, what he knows belongs in a museum of the past and is in no way suitable for the modern world.

Unfortunately a considerable number of Third World intellectuals are like our fictitious physicist; they know a great deal, but their knowledge does not extend to new areas. Not only that, but these intellectuals also continue to engage in lengthy debates in which they use obsolete terms of reference which confirm that they are living in the past, and, consequently, are unable to comprehend what is happening around them. Indeed, these obsolete frames of reference stand as obstacles in the way of society's ability to take the only means of transportation that can carry it to the desired destination, or, stated otherwise, its ability to play the game according to its new rules, not according to utopian rules that exist only in the minds of those who remain locked in the past.

Having come this far in our analysis, we cannot proceed any further without addressing an issue inextricably linked to all discussions touching upon the subject of conspiracies and the conspiracy theory, namely, once again, the Japanese phenomenon. If one believes in conspiracies, then surely there could be no conspiracy more heinous than the two atomic bombs dropped on Hiroshima and Nagasaki in 1945. For, by definition, a conspiracy seeks to inflict injury on the party against whom it is aimed, and there can be no greater injury than the atomic devastation which rained down on Japan over half a century ago.

Japan's refusal to remain locked in the spiral of defeat proves that, even assuming that a conspiracy does exist and that, moreover, it attains its full scope (that is, the infliction of maximum damage on the party against whom it is directed), the conspirators cannot achieve their ultimate aim unless the targeted victim accepts that it is to be crushed. Japan has risen like a phoenix from the ashes of the atomic blasts to become the main rival of the very powers that seemed, in 1945, to have succeeded in bringing it to its knees.

The most important thing left to say about the unshakable belief in the conspiracy theory that seems to have taken hold of the Arab mentality is that it denotes a complete denial of a number of fundamental principles which are vital to remember:

- It proceeds from the assumption that while the conspirators enjoy absolute freedom of action when it comes to exercising their will, the parties conspired against are totally devoid of that prerogative. This endows the former with the attributes of motivation, determination, will and the ability to make things happen, while stripping the parties conspired against of all these attributes, reducing them to objects rather than subjects, inanimate pawns moved on the chessboard of history according to the whims of others.
- It denies the parties conspired against the quality of nationalism while attributing it exclusively to the conspirators.

- It makes the conspirators legendary figures in the minds of those who consider themselves victims of conspiracies.
- It assumes that there is no way the parties conspired against can foil the stratagems of the conspirators, making for a defeatist and passive attitude that runs counter to pride and self-dignity, and to the notion that nations, like men, can shape their own destiny.

All that I have written about the conspiracy theory would be incomplete – as well as contrary to my beliefs – if the reader was left with the impression that, first, I believe that conspiracy and conflict are one and the same thing and that, accordingly, I do not believe that conflict has been a constant feature of human history; or, second, that I am denying that conspiracies too have always been a part of that history. In fact I am profoundly convinced that human history is made up of a series of conflicts, and moreover, that the world stage today is the setting for numerous bitter and major conflicts. But I also believe that conflict and conspiracy are two different notions. Conflict means persistent efforts by given parties to maintain whatever edge they enjoy over others, or even to expand that edge, and the privileges and advantages that go with it. But conflict also means that contradictions are played out in a game that proceeds according to certain rules which differ from one era to the next, so that whoever wants to achieve a position of any prominence must wage the conflict with the tools, and according to the rules that will guarantee the optimal results. Here the Japanese model emerges one more time, as the most salient proof of this characterization. Conflict is a relatively more open game than conspiracy; the degree of ambiguity in which the game of conflict is shrouded (even its features that are so ambiguous as to appear closer to magic than anything else) is relatively less than that necessarily surrounding the conspiracy game. Placing matters in the context of a conflict game rather than within the parameters of a tight conspiracy that determines the course of history encourages people to draw on their inner resources of pride, dignity, and determination, to enter the game as active participants bent on affecting its outcome to their advantage.

This is very different from the state of mind created by a widespread belief in the conspiracy theory as the driving force of history. This state of mind encourages people to adopt a passive attitude; they believe that they have no choice but to bow to the inevitable – albeit with much wringing of hands and loud complaints at the often disastrous results coming their way – rather than rise to the challenge by becoming active players determined to achieve honourable results in the game, even if the cards are stacked against them. The experience of the Japanese, who have waged one of the most ferocious conflicts in human history throughout the last half century, stands as a testimony to the triumph of the human spirit in the face of great adversity. Again, that is not in any way to imply that history is devoid of conspiracies; indeed, the annals of human history are rife with examples of plots and counter-plots. What I am trying to say, rather, is that history is not a general conspiracy, but the stage for a fierce and relentless struggle on which those who quietly accept whatever comes their way are relegated to the sidelines.

Finally, it is necessary here to highlight another disastrous aspect of the rampant belief in the general conspiracy theory, which is the aspect related to undemocratic rulers, like some of those now in power in the Third World. The undemocratic ruler contributes with his ideas, statements and media apparatus in consecrating the belief in the conspiracy theory. It is a useful fig-leaf behind which he can hide his own shortcomings and failures, since it allows him to put the blame of the problems and hardships faced by his people, as well as his inability to respond to their aspirations, on external elements, that is, a general conspiracy, rather than on the real reason, which is the absence of democracy, and the existence of rulers like him – who are usually far from being the most efficient, capable, honest or cultured members of the society they represent.

The real challenge is not a global conspiracy but a global conflict, one that is ferocious, violent and dangerous, which nations can only wage successfully if they are properly equipped. And they can only be equipped if their leaders are men of vision operating in a climate of democracy through cadres characterized by a high degree of efficiency, ability, honesty and culture. It is impossible to overrate the importance of this last attribute, for without culture there can be no vision.

Finally although the logic of the proponents of the conspiracy theory is based on a patriotic love of country, and they are in fact nationalists who want only the best (in their own terms) for their country and people, their absolute belief in the conspiracy theory renders them defeatists and advocates of the line of least resistance, which is to bemoan their lot as parties conspired against, without making any serious attempt to do anything about it.

A. Dealing with Conspiracy

Going beyond what has become a sterile and demobilizing debate, 'Is there a conspiracy against us?', there is a further question: 'Assuming we are in fact pawns in a grand design orchestrated by others, is there anything we can do other than lament the fact, which so many seem to think is the only course open to us?'

In fact, the reaction to the conspiracy – assuming it exists – can be any of several scenarios. The first is embodied in the reaction of the majority of our conspiracy theorists; it is to rant against the conspirators and speechifying about how much they hate and envy us. This becomes an occasion to enumerate the qualities that make us an object of envy. I call this the 'declamatory scenario'. Then there is the 'confrontation scenario', in which the self-perceived 'victims' of a conspiracy adopt a confrontational stance towards the 'conspirators'.

Finally there is what I have chosen to call the 'Asian scenario', after something said to me by a prominent Japanese citizen. He asked me why the Middle East was so obsessed with conspiracies and conspirators, in contrast with East and Southeast Asia. He continued, 'Despite the atomic bombs dropped by the West on our cities, we did not waste our time talking about conspiracies. Instead of indulging in this futile exercise, we directed our attention at building ourselves up internally in all spheres, economic, political, social, educational and cultural. We opted for action rather than words, because we realized that the declamatory scenario would get us nowhere: it would neither benefit us nor hurt others. As to the confrontational scenario, setting ourselves on a collision course with the West would have exacted a heavy price, and we would have ended up squandering our time, assets, resources and energy striving for the impossible.'

The Asian scenario, which eschews words in favour of action, was adopted by China in another, very different, matter. Instead of becoming bogged down in an endless debate over the respective merits of a socialist command economy based on centralized planning versus a market economy, China quietly pressed ahead with its own version of the Asian scenario, keeping most of its provinces under the old system while allowing a few to follow a market economy. After what had started out as a limited experiment which proved to be successful, China gradually expanded its scope, moving smoothly from the old economic system to the new one. Thus it did not tear society apart by involving it in a polarizing and endless national debate which would have sent the pro- and anti-change camps at each other's throats and sapped the national will, hampering it from moving forward. Too much talk and no action can only erode society's resolve and, as the old adage goes, 'it is a nation's resolve that can revive it'.

The Japanese speaker went on:

> Look at China, which is theoretically more dangerous for the West – approximately a thousand times more dangerous – than you are. And yet, it avoided getting bogged down in useless talk about conspiracies, and it focused on the process of building itself up from within. I believe that Russia and India, like China, also represent a greater threat to the West than the Arabs do, and yet neither of them got caught up in a war of words against conspiracies and conspirators. This tends to prove that you, Arabs, are using this talk about conspiracy for other reasons; maybe an inability to deal with what is essentially a conflict situation as active participants bent on affecting the outcome to their advantage, which entails building a strong, healthy, stable and thriving internal environment.

That talk about conspiracy can be as demobilizing for a society as talk of the clash of civilizations. Even if we assume, for the sake of argument, that we are the targets of a conspiracy, we should ask ourselves what positive action we can take to foil the designs of the conspirators. Loudly bewailing our fate while waiting passively for whatever they decide to throw at us hardly qualifies as positive action. At best, the declamatory scenario is the line of least resistance, a static scenario that locks us into a world of fiery language, and prevents us from taking control of our destiny.

If we opt for the confrontational scenario, we must be ready to pay a heavy price in terms of our financial, natural, economic and human resources. In the final analysis, then, it is only by adopting the Asian scenario based on building a strong internal front in all fields, political, economic, social, educational and cultural, that we can hope to achieve our aim, namely serving this nation and ensuring a better future for coming generations. The point I am trying to make can best be summed up as follows: the source of any country's pride is in its ability to realize its goals. It is a statement that could be made to counter the declamatory and confrontational scenarios. The former, in which words take the place of deeds, is incapable of achieving pride, while the latter, in the absence of a strong internal front, can only result in great loss.

It would be easy to convince most people in the region of how ineffectual the declamatory scenario is when it comes to coping with external threats. It is a familiar scenario which has consistently failed to live up to its extravagant promises. It has all too often led to situations for which we were ill-prepared, with disastrous consequences. But while most people who realize that 'big talk' has cost us dearly would be receptive to the idea that the declamatory scenario is no longer an option, they would be less ready to concede that the confrontational scenario too should be abandoned. In fact there are those who would challenge my contention that the confrontational scenario can only be a losing, defeatist proposition.

This challenge can easily be rebutted; even the most fervent believers in a conspiracy theory cannot deny that our internal front is weak and friable, and that all our resources must be deployed to address this problem. Neither can they deny that overcoming the problem entails a concerted effort that combines scientific knowledge, modern management techniques, a serious programme for reform and development, an educational revolution aimed at bringing the region's educational system into line with modern educational systems (which are based on creativity not memory tests), expanding the scope of general freedoms and allowing for wider popular participation in public affairs. If we can easily reach an agreement on this point, we should just as easily be able to agree that embarking on a confrontational scenario for which we are not prepared will cost us dearly.

Thus building a strong internal front is the first task because it is the only way to deal effectively with the outside world, whether as partners in a state of peaceful coexistence, or as protagonists in a confrontational situation. Neither coexistence nor confrontation is possible unless we focus on improving our internal structural reform.

In this connection a useful lesson can be drawn from the experience of Muhammad Ali. As long as he confined himself to building Egypt's internal institutions, he was neither subjected to any external pressure nor dragged into confrontations aimed at clipping his wings. But when he shifted his attention from the internal front, and began harbouring ambitions to transform Egypt into a great power with an important role to play and interests to promote beyond its borders, he found himself facing the same fate as that of countless dedicated rulers who succumbed to the temptation of expanding their sphere of influence beyond the borders of their own countries. Even assuming, for the sake of argument, that there *is* a conspiracy, there are still tremendous dangers in opting for the declamatory or confrontational scenarios. The former serves only to paralyze society; the latter, while feeding the psychological cravings of some, satisfying the emotional needs of others and responding to the basic instincts of many, can only deplete our resources and cause us to incur heavy losses we can ill afford. As it is said, pride can only come from success, and there is nothing worse than allowing what is attainable to slip from our grasp while we strive for the unattainable!

III. BELIEF IN STEREOTYPES

Another essential step towards success is to get rid of the tendency to blindly accept and follow 'stereotypes'. Actually the English word 'stereotypes' has no equivalent in Arabic, but is usually translated into two words (*al-afkar al-namatiyya*), literally meaning 'standardized ideas'. The word 'cliché', though commonly used in colloquial Arabic, is originally French. By stereotypes, I mean the hackneyed expressions people use in a more or less automatic fashion without stopping to think what they really mean, that is, without exercising their critical faculties to determine whether these expressions are right or wrong and, accordingly, whether they should accept or reject them. It is, of course, easier to unquestioningly accept generally held ideas than to exert the mind searching for the deeper meaning behind them.

A common feature of human behaviour that exists to varying degrees in all societies, stereotyping is an extremely negative phenomenon that does nothing to foster greater understanding between peoples. Many of the West's perceptions of other societies, civilizations and cultures are based on stereotypes; and we too are guilty of perceiving the 'Other' through the prism of stereotypes which acquire an aura of truth through endless repetition. The universal tendency to accept stereotypes at face value rather than subject them to critical examination is a triumph of rhetoric over reasoning. While this tendency is part of human nature and, as such, can never be completely eradicated, I believe steps can be taken to limit its spread.

To that end it might be useful to try and identify the main reasons for the profusion of stereotypes that have come to dominate people's perceptions in today's world. I believe there are four main sources for the phenomenon. The first is the lack of knowledge that can serve as a shield against the blind acceptance of stereotypes. The second is the absence of what I believe to be the main enemy of stereotypes, namely, a free and uninterrupted dialogue. The third is the lack of a human dimension in the process of globalization currently sweeping the world, which proceeds from an economic/political premise with little regard for humanistic/cultural considerations. The fourth is a psychology dominated by a defensive mentality. I will try to explain each of these four sources before moving on to the intellectual tools by which I believe the phenomenon of stereotypes can be challenged.

The first source from which the phenomenon springs can be found in societies where the store of knowledge forming the intellectual sensibility of the population in general and of the educated and cultured elite in particular, can be characterized as either limited, flimsy or insular, and hence inhospitable to opinions deviating from the norm. Even though some members of the educated and cultured elite could have a reasonably rich store of knowledge on which to draw, their frames of reference are often rooted in the past, whether a distant past stretching back for centuries or a more recent past going back only a few decades. As a result their approach to questions of the day does not take into account modern developments in various fields of knowledge, especially in the fields of social science.

Many are the intellectuals, especially in the Third World, whose store of knowledge belongs more to the 1950s and 1960s than to the present. Many are those who are imprisoned in a mentality that is incapable of breaking free of the shackles of parochialism to explore wider horizons. In some cases, these intellectuals may display a store of knowledge that is rich in some aspects and poor in others, notably in the area of modern social sciences. Thus the existence of a store of knowledge (for the ordinary citizens as well as for the educated elite) that can be characterized as strong, non-parochial and capable of expanding into new areas, is society's only shield from the spread of stereotypes and biases. In such a context critical faculties can develop and allow people to choose between several alternatives rather than to accept stereotypes blindly as the line of least resistance.

The second source for the phenomenon of stereotypes can be found in societies whose educational and cultural constructs are not built on a solid foundation of dialogue. When educational techniques rely on rote learning and memory tests, when relationships in the world of education and in society at large are based on monologues (transmitters and receivers) and not on dialogue, this creates an ideal climate for the propagation of stereotypes. The opposite is true: dialogue is an effective tool by which their propagation can be limited.

The third source is the failure by the advocates of globalization to give a humanistic/cultural face to a project that has so far succeeded in portraying itself exclusively in economic/political terms. There is a pressing need to introduce a human dimension to globalization in order to allay the fears of many in the less developed parts of the world who regard it as a device to promote the interests of others at their expense, or worse, as a weapon designed to destroy the structural underpinnings of their societies, whether political, economic or cultural. As one who has no problem recognizing that the West, where the notion of globalization was born, is firmly ensconced in the driving seat of progress in every sense of the word, I am convinced that the introduction of these two equally important dimensions, humanistic and cultural, to the globalization process is the responsibility of the West. I also believe that one of the main reasons for this serious deficiency is that global leadership is now in the hands of the United States.

In fact it is not only the concept of globalization that suffers from this deficiency: the same is true of such other vital notions in today's world as 'human rights', 'general freedoms' and 'democracy'. The West, which has developed these notions in its own societies, needs to add a humanistic dimension to their application by dealing with them as universal (rather than regional) values whose sovereignty extends to the whole of humanity. Otherwise the West will continue to be accused of applying a double standard. Worse, it will render these values meaningless for those in the underdeveloped world who hear that they exist in the West, but have seen nothing in the last fifty years to indicate that the West is overly concerned with extending their benefits to the rest of the world. I believe that the failure to develop the globalization process in such a way as to place humanistic/cultural needs on the same footing as economic/political considerations is one of the main sources for the propagation of stereotypes.

The fourth and final source is a general psychological climate characterized by a perceived need to adopt a posture of self-defence. A sense of achievement and progress renders the members of any society less susceptible to two things: the need to be on the defensive, and the feeling that they are victims of a conspiracy. These two factors create an ideal climate for stereotypes, which are usually used by people to cover their feelings of inadequacy, and shift the blame for their society's lack of progress from where it rightfully belongs on to the shoulders of others.

These then are the main sources of stereotypes. While it may be impossible to eradicate the phenomenon altogether, given that it exists in all societies to one degree or another, there are mechanisms by which its insidious spread can be reduced to manageable proportions. The most effective mechanism is education: curricula, philosophy, teachers and the general learning environment.

Only education can plant such values as pluralism in society; only education can form critical minds that require proof before accepting the truth of any proposition; only education can imbue people with a sense of the primacy of reason, so that they test any idea through a reasoning process rather than through ensuring its conformity with set formulas. These are the tools which can limit the spread of a culture of stereotypes. However, in the short and the medium term, the media can be more effective in exposing the incoherence and intellectual shallowness of stereotypes. They can also show the link between a culture of stereotypes and other misconceptions like the 'big talk' syndrome, the tendency to indulge in self-praise and the irrational belief in conspiracy theories; for there can be no denying the existence of a dialectical relationship between all these negative phenomena.

NOTES

1. In November 1947 UN Resolution 181 was adopted by the majority of the members of the General Assembly of the UN, according to which the international community endorsed the partition of historic Palestine into two distinct entities: a Jewish state and an Arab state. The Resolution was opposed by the Arab members of the UN.
2. Mountainous region in the south of Lebanon of high strategic importance. Israel captured the Golan Heights from Syria during the 1967 Six Day War. The territory was successfully defended by Israel in the 1973 Yom Kippur War though a portion was later returned to Syria. The Golan Heights remain disputed.
3. 123 out of 182 (see http://hdrstats.undp.org/en/countries/country_fact_sheets/cty_fs_EGY.html).
4. The Crusades were the Christian-driven military campaigns that originated in Europe against the Muslim-dominated territories of the Near East, especially Palestine (the Holy Land). The campaigns and invasions took part between the end of the eleventh through to the thirteenth century. Their main objective was to save those territories from what was perceived as a Muslim desecration and to restore Christian control there. In modern times

the Crusades have come to symbolize in some Muslim/Arab circles Western aggression, colonialism and imperialism in the area, of which the State of Israel is considered to be the gravest manifestation.

5. The Ministry of Information is found in many Arab countries. Among its responsibilities are the regulation and control of State and non-governmental media. In many cases the same Ministry also acts as the government's main official mouthpiece.
6. Zionism was the movement seeking the creation of an independent national Jewish home in Palestine or Israel. The movement originated in the late nineteenth century among eastern European Jewry. From 1896 the term was adopted by Theodor Herzl (1860–1904) for the political movement founded by him and which eventually led to the formation of the State of Israel.

13

The Victims[1]

One of the worst misconceptions of Arab culture hampering progress is reflected in the way minorities are perceived in the Arab societies. The conditions of these minorities are far from enviable. First there is the status of women in the majority of the Arabic-speaking countries; then there is the status of other ethnic or religious minorities, such as the Shia in Saudi Arabia and the Copts in Egypt.

I. WOMEN, THE GENDER MINORITY

I write to save women from the cells of tyrants
from the cities of the dead
from the state of polygamy
from the monotony of days
the ice, the repetitiveness.[2]

Nizar Qabbani

Our intention to establish the values of progress cannot be fulfilled unless we all feel most ashamed of the manner women were and are treated in many societies, where they were or are to a shameful degree denied most of their human rights. The patriarchal 'dominant male' culture is a disgrace to mankind; if men apologized to women for a thousand years it would still be 'insufficient'. This will seem undeniable to some Westerners, but in the Middle East (and elsewhere) we need thousands of voices and wills to weaken the prevailing medieval masculine culture.

Women's status in most Arab societies is in dire need of serious review. Not only do women constitute half of the population, but also their societal role, because of the influence they wield as mothers, is far greater than their numbers. Unfortunately, the status they are accorded in no way reflects this reality. To redress the situation, it is necessary to stop ignoring it and acknowledge the real problem. By breaking out of the denial mentality, it is possible to make a critical appraisal of the situation before developing concrete policies designed to enhance the status of Arab women in line with what they deserve and with the requirements of the age.

Here the wall of denial is at its highest; we are constantly congratulating ourselves on how well women are treated in our culture, and how they are given rights not enjoyed by their sisters in the West. The example most often cited to prove this point is their independent patrimony. We also hold up exceptional (and symbolic) cases in which women achieved prominence as proof of the equality enjoyed by women as a whole, a myth we are able to perpetuate thanks to our amazing ability to hide behind the impenetrable wall of denial.

One of the most important indicators of a society's progress is the status it accords to women and how they are perceived in the prevailing cultural climate. Indeed, that is perhaps one of the most accurate ways to measure the extent of a society's progress or backwardness. This cause of equal rights for women is so important because a society that subordinates women to men cannot hope to make any headway on the path to progress. The institutionalized concept of male superiority works against the interests of not only women as a group but also society as a whole. In other words the worst thing about male chauvinism is not that it is reactionary and completely out of step with the spirit of the age, or even that it is at odds with basic human rights, but that it is an insurmountable obstacle in the way of progress.

Male chauvinism grows from the seeds of male insecurity. A confident man who believes in himself, his intellect and his abilities, having a strong sense of self, does not need to assert his superiority over women. Experience shows that the more modest a man's capabilities, the more insistent he is on clinging to the chauvinistic culture that relegates women to a lower status than men. It is understandable, as those who fail at the public level have nothing left but to assert themselves artificially in their little private domain.

Strangely enough the generations that grew up in the 1950s and 1960s are more progressive on this issue than subsequent generations. Several factors have contributed to this phenomenon. One is the spread of reactionary interpretations of religious teachings; another is the higher-profile role that was being assumed by women. With more and more women receiving an education and participating in the workforce, the myth of male superiority was effectively shattered. To compensate for this blow to their self-esteem, many young men sought refuge in a kind of mythical victory, invoking their innate superiority on no other grounds than their gender.

Some of the proponents of the male-superiority theory use specious arguments to back their claim that women are somehow inferior to men, often citing religious texts to justify their position. But there are always other texts that assert the full humanity of women and the equality of both sexes.[3] At the end of the day, any text, even if it is divine, requires a human agency to interpret it, and the real test is how the mind elects to deal with it. Thus the source for the notion of male superiority is not, as some people claim, religion, but the stages of human history in general, and of tribal/Bedouin history in particular, when civilization and humanistic values were at low ebb.

Religion, although used by proponents of male chauvinism, has nothing to do with the issue, as exemplified by the first marriage of the Prophet. Both partners were equal; for example, the wife had the right to divorce, and the husband did not take a second wife. But the reactionary chauvinists choose to ignore these examples.

The first person in history to receive the Nobel Prize more than once was Madame Curie.[4] That alone is enough to silence those who claim that men are superior to women, and it is far from being the only instance of public recognition of a woman's excellent achievements. But diehard male chauvinists dismiss the argument that brilliant women like Madame Curie, who are light years ahead of them in intelligence, knowledge and success, testify to the fallacy of the male superiority theory, and they claim that such women are exceptions that confirm the rule. In fact, the only reason for which women were not allowed to realize their full potential earlier is that, for centuries, they were subjugated to men, who then claimed they were unfit to take part in, let alone win, the race. Possibly because they were driven by a sense of challenge and the desire to prove themselves, women often proved to be superior in many ways.

Women's organizations have worked and continue to work tirelessly to promote the status of women in society. Yet they are required to do even more, to set in place a comprehensive plan designed to put an end to the reactionary male chauvinist culture dominating our society – in the family, in education, in religious institutions and in the media. A campaign should be launched to drive home the point that the only source of a man's blind belief in his innate superiority over the opposite sex is a tremendous lack of self-confidence. Free people like to deal with free people, and the opposite is true. The only men I hear propounding outlandish theories about their superiority over women and the inability of women to hold leadership positions are frustrated men who are themselves devoid of any qualities of leadership or elements of superiority.

Any society that views women as unequal to men contrives to find references and 'evidence' to support its perception, although the attitude has no religious or legal basis, but is a purely cultural phenomenon. It follows that the more developed a society's educational/cultural environment, the less inclined its members are to subscribe to the primitive belief that a person's worth is determined by gender. In a developed society, people no longer need to ask the question that is reactionary by its very nature, namely, 'are women equal to men?' There are clear examples that prove that the issue in its entirety is a cultural one.

Despite the existence of Quranic texts enjoining men to release a wife who no longer wishes to continue the marital relationship and prohibiting them from keeping her against her will just to hurt her, the legal system has for many years provided men with a legal device that allows them to do the exact opposite: the infamous *bayt al-ta'a.* This terrible mechanism adopted by some Islamic jurists allows police to force the wife to stay with her husband regardless of her will.

Therefore there can be no doubt that the *khul* law enacted on 1 March 2000 by the Egyptian government and which allows a woman to unilaterally repudiate a marriage, represents an important step forward. It makes use of a mechanism in Islamic jurisprudence that allows women to get divorced against the will of the spouse – with a number of financial consequences and burdens. When this mechanism was legally introduced in Egypt, it was faced with a strong wave of opposition from the conservative segment of the society.

But this law will remain vulnerable unless legal and constitutional guarantees are put in place in order to foil attempts by reactionary forces to have it repealed. For although the system of *bayt al-ta'a* was a disgraceful legal, social and cultural travesty, when the government enacted the *khul* law, merely empowering women to exercise a human right that no fair-minded person can oppose, it stuck in the throats of thousands of our men. How could the law deprive them of a tool of brutal injustice that was in their hands? If they had a reasonable amount of self-confidence, this long overdue legal development, which represents a very important step forward, would not have bothered them at all.

One can only wonder how a man who wants the law to help him keep his wife locked in a marriage against her will can reconcile his attitude with such values as manliness, chivalry and honour. The long and glorious history of Arab male chivalry, decency and pride is rendered meaningless when a man keeps his wife in a marital relationship which she does not want. The issue is also indicative of a state of cultural rot when thousands of young men and women are completely opposed to the idea of granting women the right to divorce, even though it was a right held by the first wife of the Prophet himself.

Nevertheless progress should not stop at the promulgation of the *khul* law. To sustain the momentum, more steps need to be taken. For example, a provision should be included in the marriage contract to invest the wife with the right to obtain a divorce. More generally it is essential to promote a cultural climate conducive to the adoption of a standard marriage contract drafted along the lines of the one which was referred to above, which the Prophet Muhammad and his first wife, Khadija bint Khuwaylad, entered into, and which stipulated that she could terminate the contract at any time, and that he would not take a second wife.

Another equally important step forward has been the appointment of the first female judge to Egypt's Supreme Constitutional Court. But again our appreciation for what is undoubtedly a commendable – if long overdue – development should not blind us to the fact that it is only a small dent in the armour of a strong patriarchal culture; this step needs to be followed up. The Ministry of Justice needs to sustain this forward momentum by appointing women to at least 25 per cent of the positions of deputy public prosecutors. The appointment of women to all levels of the judicial system is the only way to end what is an affront to the norms of civilized behavior. A society that restricts important positions to men uses up only half of its potential of intelligence, performance, productivity and education; it is a society running on half power. Not surprisingly a society that does not make full use of all its assets remains in a state of underdevelopment for how can a person run on one foot?

It is not only the judicial system that needs to open its doors to women. The executive branch could put a programme in place aimed at appointing a large number of women as governors, deputy governors, university presidents, faculty deans and city council heads; in short to all the public positions from which they are still excluded. In the absence of a concerted effort in that direction, proponents of the male superiority theory and other reactionary forces will have the opportunity to wipe out the progressive steps recently taken to enhance the status of women. Enacting these decisions as a fait accompli is the only way to prevent the cultural setback which our society would suffer if the *khul* law was repealed and if the appointment of women to prominent positions was challenged.

A most shocking aspect of the male supremacist mentality that has taken hold in some societies is that this mentality is not, as might have been supposed, confined to the male segment of the population. Although men are its source and beneficiaries, the myth is embraced wholeheartedly by many girls and women, who raise their children to accept without question propositions that run counter to all contemporary values of progress, science and civilization.

It is impossible to liberate women from the yoke of the male supremacist culture, which is a form of slavery, unless women themselves are at the vanguard of a movement to change societal attitudes for these to be in line with the requirements of the age; and to replace the reactionary view that women are inferior beings with a view that accepts them as equal to men in all respects. Moreover, they should promote the notion that although they constitute half of the population, their actual value, as mothers, is far greater than their mere numbers. It is tragic that in this day and age, when the advanced world is concerned with knowledge, development, civil liberties and human rights, we should still be asking the shameful question: 'Are women equal to men?'

Those who are today expounding reactionary ideas in the name of religion are worthy successors of those who attributed socialism to Islam in the 1960s only to say the exact opposite a few years later. They are reminiscent, too, of those who, after years of telling us that war with Israel was a religious duty for Muslims, suddenly decided in the 1970s that Islam enjoined us to make peace with this country, invoking a religious text to support their new pacifism: 'If they lean towards peace, so too should you.'[5] They are the same people who invoked religion to justify the infamous practice of breaking the will of recalcitrant wives by locking them up in the so-called 'house of obedience' (*bayt al-ta'a*) and then reversed their position.

To these people we say that we know as much about Islamic jurisprudence as they do and that one of the first things we learned is that Islamic jurisprudence is defined as the extrapolation of judicial rulings from available legal proof; in other words through a process of deductive reasoning that involves a human agency. This was best expressed by the great Islamic jurist Abu Hanifa in his description of Islamic jurisprudence as 'a science of opinions, so that if someone comes forward with a better opinion we accept it.'[6]

The conclusion to be drawn from a thorough reading of the thousands of reference works on Islamic jurisprudence is that it is a human science initially established by great thinkers. These were followed by the strict traditionalists who spurned deductive reasoning altogether and insisted on a dogmatic adherence to scripture. With their limited knowledge and lack of intellectual abilities these so-called 'expositors' invested the purely human field of Islamic jurisprudence with a divine character.

The time has come to break the institutionalized concept of male superiority that colours the general attitude toward women in our society. To that end, measures must be taken to safeguard the steps already taken in that direction and to prevent anyone from engineering a cultural setback in the future. For, at the end of the day, the notion that men are innately superior to women is deeply entrenched in the cultural tissue of society. It is only by recognizing the existence of an organic link between people's cultural formation and the beliefs they hold that we can understand and properly address the mentality that seeks to keep women at the same lowly status to which they have been relegated throughout much of our history.

The use of religion to justify this view is a political cover for fossilized societal attitudes deriving from the following sources: Bedouin customs, medieval values and a patriarchal culture that is deeply rooted in tribal society. What can we expect of men who have drunk deeply from these sources and who, moreover, have never drunk from the well of universal human culture? Men whose inability to master the linguistic tools of the Renaissance keeps them isolated from the great masterpieces of human creativity?

This cultural insularity makes the absence of objectivity on the issue of women's rights absolute. We are facing a situation where revisionism prevails coupled with primitiveness collared by a tribal mentality and covered with a layer of cultural isolation from the masterpieces of universal human culture. The situation is rendered even more intractable by the fact that men are clinging to the myth of their superiority over women out of a tremendous lack of self-confidence, a sense that they must at all costs defend themselves against what they see as a challenge to their supremacy.

There is a need to grant women full equality with men from both perspectives: as a prerequisite for society's progress and as a basic human right. The two aspects are not mutually exclusive; they complement one another.

II. RELIGIOUS MINORITIES

Another flagrant human rights violation and obstacle to progress in the Arab societies is manifested in the treatment of religious minorities. The Shia of the Arabian Peninsula and the Copts of Egypt are obvious examples and are certainly not the only ones. Yet the similarity in the treatment of both minorities is striking even though one is Muslim and the other Christian and both live in different countries.

The Shia in the Kingdom of Saudi Arabia, for instance, are oppressed to the extent of being denied any official or ministerial positions. Also, in spite of living in areas rich with oil, public services are not extended to them, and they live in poor conditions. Moreover, they are denied the right of building houses of worship even at their own expense and the religious rituals of their cult are totally neglected througout the entire Kingdom. Furthermore they are defamed by the Wahhabis who not only incite hatred against the Shia but also proclaim them enemies of the nation and allow all sorts of evils to be perpetrated against them.

The tragic parallel in Egypt is seen in the Copts, who are denied access to certain high positions, are deprived of the freedom to build new churches, and suffer from increasingly suffocating fanaticism from all directions. The basic premise is that the Copts are (or should be) genuine Egyptian citizens, that is, first-class citizens. Egypt is their country; they are not living there by the grace of others but are fully entitled to enjoy the status and rights of nationhood as full partners, not as charity cases.

If this premise is disputed there can be no dialogue. Those who regard Egyptians of the Coptic faith as second-class citizens allowed to live in the country thanks only to tolerance and magnanimity, or those who call for the imposition of the *jizya* (the poll-tax required of non-Muslims) on members of the Coptic community, are not going to be convinced.

The basic issue is: 'Do the Copts in Egypt suffer from serious problems in their own country?' The only possible answer is: 'Yes.' Yes, Copts fear for themselves, their families, their property and their safety much more than Muslims do, though the latter, too, are not completely safe. Yes, Copts suffer from a public atmosphere of fanaticism characterized by severe animosity toward them.

A major grievance over which there is complete consensus within the Coptic community is that the right to construct new churches or restore old ones has until recently been severely curtailed by legislative and bureaucratic constraints. Although these constraints have been somewhat eased, most Copts believe the situation is still far from satisfactory. The only way out of this untenable situation is to unify the laws governing the construction and restoration of all houses of worship, whether they are called mosques or churches. These laws should lay down a set of rational rules applicable to all Egyptians, regardless of creed. For it is totally illogical that one segment of society should be subjected to arbitrary constraints while another is allowed to enjoy unbridled freedom when it comes to constructing places of worship or congregating to offer prayer when and where its members choose. Indeed, and it is often the case, even when this leads to chaotic situations involving violations of law, people are too intimidated to challenge the offenders, leaving them free to flout the law with impunity.

But while this is a major grievance, it is far from being the only, or even the main, reason for the widespread feeling among Egypt's Christians that they are living in a tense moment, not to say a crisis situation:

- The existence of a general climate that allows for the resurgence of a spirit of religious intolerance at different times and in certain areas of the country. Copts are finely attuned to this phenomenon, as sometimes the mere mention of their name is enough to trigger a hostile reaction.
- There is a widespread feeling among Copts that their participation in public life has gradually dwindled over the last fifty years.

Their sense of marginalization is borne out by the facts, as in 1995 when not a single Copt was elected to parliament.
- There is, moreover, the spectre of communal violence, which can flare up at any time as it has done in the past, most notably in the Koshh incident. Koshh is a village in Upper Egypt in which hostility from rigid and intolerant Muslims broke out more than once and ended in 1999 with a massacre in which more than twenty Copts were murdered.

First, with regard to the general climate which breeds a spirit of hateful fanaticism, this did not come about by a governmental decree or a political decision but was a natural result of the defeat of the Egyptian revival project, especially after the June 1967 debacle. The vacuum was quickly filled by a fundamentalist ideology and culture, which put itself forward as an alternative to the movement for a new Egyptian awakening. With the spread of the cultural values of this trend (whose members committed many crimes, most notably the assassination of Anwar Sadat) the general climate fell prey to the forces of conservatism and regression, which inevitably bred a context of hostility toward the Copts.

As a noted Egyptian intellectual once put it, whenever the revival project is defeated in Egypt, there are negative repercussions on two groups of Egyptians: women and Copts. The opposite is equally true; in a vital and dynamic cultural climate the attitude toward these two groups is enlightened and in keeping with the values of civilization and progress. It may be unfair to blame the current regime for creating an environment which breeds fanaticism and allows the resurgence of religious intolerance, with the attendant risk of communal violence. However, it is a fact that the government could have done, and can still do much to limit the dangerous polarization that has come to characterize the cultural climate in Egypt today.

To that end, it could adopt a policy aimed at the positive reinforcement of a culture of religious tolerance to replace the spirit of fanaticism threatening us all. While educational curricula and the media are the right place to start, we must not forget the importance of religious pulpits in shaping public perceptions. For there can be no hope of progress if Islamic religious institutions oppose a cultural project aimed at eradicating the spirit of religious intolerance which has taken hold in our society. This is why *al-Azhar* must follow the vision of the regime, not the other way round. To leave matters to the men of religion is to accept the spread of a theocratic culture; logic and experience prove that theocracy cannot possibly support a culture of tolerance and acceptance of the right of others to differ; neither can it accept the notion of unity through diversity. All this is easier said than done, and the Egyptian government faces a daunting challenge. But the role of any leadership is to formulate a vision and to work toward achieving it. In order to succeed, they must lead and not allow themselves to be led. It would be wrong to claim that the regime is by its nature unwilling to face up to the challenge or that it is responsible for creating the ugly spirit of fanaticism that has come to pervade our society. It has, however, turned a blind eye to this aberration for a long time, only slowly coming to the realization that the ideology behind the culture of fanaticism is the main enemy of the regime. It is this ideology which spawned the assassins of Anwar Sadat, the would-be assassins of the Addis Ababa incident, and the perpetrators of many other crimes.[7]

Second the widespread feeling among Copts that their representation in public life has shrunk considerably over the last few decades is borne out by official statistics, but this should not be seen as a deliberate attempt by the regime to keep Copts out of public office. It should rather be regarded as a negative phenomenon that grew insidiously over the years, unnoticed by successive governments and driven by its own dynamics, until it reached its present unacceptable proportions. But whatever the reason, the fact remains that the Copts are marginalized in Egyptian public life.

To claim, as some do, that the situation is of the Copts' own making, that they have become marginalized because they are too passive and too taken up in financial activities, is to put the cart before the horse. Copts are passive and involved in financial and economic activities because other opportunities are closed to them, despite their undeniable abilities. The same opportunities denied to highly qualified members of the Coptic community remain closed to many highly qualified members of the Egyptian society in general. The political game in Egypt today is open only to those willing to play by certain rules established over the last few decades based on personal loyalty, nepotism and other mechanisms having nothing to do with professional abilities.

Third, the gravity of the violent communal clashes which flare up from time to time is officially played down in the mistaken belief that admitting to the existence of such a problem would be detrimental to Egypt's reputation. In fact, Egypt's reputation would be better served by confronting the issue head on rather than pretending it doesn't exist.

There has also been a failure to utilize the many worthwhile efforts made to study and analyze the root causes of such incidents, such as the famous report put out by Dr Gamal Oteify, minister of culture under President Sadat, on the spate of communal clashes which broke out in the 1970s.[8] His findings and recommendations could have been put to good use had it not been for a cultural propensity to dismiss the clashes as a minor problem instigated by external forces for the purpose of destabilizing Egypt.

To accuse the government of persecuting the Copts would be both illogical and unwise. But it would equally be illogical and unwise to pretend the Copts have no legitimate grievances and that their situation is ideal. Therefore to accuse anyone who speaks of these matters of being an agent of parties hostile to Egypt, or of being involved in a plot against Egypt, is simply a bad joke, an insult to the truth, and an affront to reason, a reflection of the style of the security services' investigations department, which tends to abandon the heart of the matter and pursue marginal issues related to personalities, suspicions and conspiratorial thinking.

This security-service mentality is one of the factors that contributed to the collapse of objectivity and rationality in our thinking and which meant that this outlook became so far removed from objective and civilized modes of analysis, which are one of the achievements of human civilization; its time has passed.

I was visited a few years ago by a person whose high-level position and job had direct bearing on the Coptic issue; he asked me why I was so enthusiastically involved in 'the Coptic issue'. I told him at the time that as an Egyptian, it was my obligation to contribute, and this was also what made me support women's issues in Egypt – because Egypt, which is sick today, will never get on the road to recovery so long as Copts and women do not contribute to addressing Egypt's problems from a position of full and unimpaired citizenship. An oppressed person whose rights are denied cannot participate in pushing forward the broken wagon. I was sure that this visitor did not understand what I told him because he had been trained to treat the Copts as a threat to Egypt, despite the fact that they are the original Egyptians.

At the time I also told him:

> If the Coptic issue is not discussed here, in Egypt, it will eventually be discussed abroad, and if we don't recognize all the aspects of the problem, then the Copts abroad will take their cause from the stage of merely crying out that they are being oppressed, to the stage of calling it a human rights issue; then, many will pay attention to them on an international level, including important decision-makers.

When I was young, I heard the Arab adage, 'Most fires start from tiny sparks that people overlooked.' Today we realize that most troubles result from their having been ignored when they were small. We demand from the world that they believe our claim of being above reproach in our treatment of non-Muslims and women, and we relish repeating this, while the world looks at our deeds and finds them to be totally contrary to what we say.

In the course of a debate on the Coptic question someone asked me what the needs and demands of the Copts were. I began with their second demand, and then moved on to the third, fourth and fifth. But what, he asked, is their first demand? I replied that what they needed above all was a 'social embrace': being made to feel that there is a genuine desire to listen to them and hear their complaints and problems based on the belief that they are equal partners in this land, not second-class citizens belonging to a minority that has to accept and bow to the will of the majority.

NOTES

1. For more of the author's writings on the suffering of minorities (like women, the Copts in Egypt and the Shiites of the Gulf region) visit his website available at www.tarek-heggy.com.
2. Author's translation from Arabic.
3. The Holy Quran, On superiority of men: Surat *Al-Nisa'* (Sura 4: 34–5); Surat *Al-Baqarah* (Sura 2) (2:282); Surat *Al-Nisa'* (Sura 4) (4:11). On equality of sexes: Surat *Al-Baqarah* (Sura 2) (2:228); Surat *Al-Nisa'* (Sura 4) (4:1); Surat *Al-Nisa'* (Sura 4) (4:7).
4. 1867–1934. Born Maria Sklodowska, physicist and chemist of Polish origin and French citizenship. The only person to win the Nobel Prize in two different disciplines: for Physics in 1903 and Chemistry in 1911.
5. The Holy Quran, Surat *al-Anfal* (Sura 8) (8:61): 'And if they incline to peace, then incline to it and trust in Allah; surely He is the Hearing, the Knowing.'
6. Abu Hanifa, *Al-Fiqh al-Akbar* [The Great Jurisprudence] (Santa Barbara, CA: White Thread Press, 2007).
7. Assassination of Egyptian President Sadat in 1981, attempt on the life of Egyptian President Mubarak in Addis Ababa in June 1995.

8. *Taqrir al lajna al mushakala min majlis al shaab letaqassi haqaeq ahdath al khanka fi november 1972 bi riassat al doctor Gamal al-Oteify* [The Report of the Committee Formed by the Assembly of the People to Investigate the Truths about the Khanka Events in November 1972, Headed by Dr Gamal Oteify], available at http://www.scribd.com/doc/7169782/-.

14

The Reality that Arabs Neglect

When the Second World War broke out in September 1939 the United States adopted a neutral stance despite the efforts made by Britain's wartime prime minister, Winston Churchill, to drag it in on the side of the Allies. The United States only entered the war in December 1941, following the Japanese attack on its naval base in Pearl Harbour.[1] US industrial and military power provided the Allies with the main strength necessary to stem the tide of initial Axis successes in Europe and the Far East and, finally, to bring the war to a victorious conclusion in the summer of 1945.

Although its intervention was the decisive factor in the Allied victory, the United States did not capitalize on this fact in the immediate aftermath of the war but delayed calling in its debt for just less than half a century. Following the logic of power politics the United States should have reaped the fruits of the victory that it was instrumental in achieving right after the war ended, but fate intervened in the form of the Cold War, which began in 1945 and lasted until 1991. During that period, the United States was locked in a battle for global supremacy with the Soviet Union, which stood as a formidable obstacle between the United States and its dream of unchallenged domination of the post-war world order. With the collapse of the Soviet Union and its satellite states, the moment for which the United States had been waiting since 1945 finally arrived. It was now free to stake its claim to global leadership on the strength not only of its victory in both the Second World War and the Cold War, but also of its uncontested political, economic, scientific and military superiority.

However its emergence as the unique superpower on the world stage, which had already been delayed by the Cold War, was even further delayed by Bill Clinton's accession to power in January 1993. Under his administration America held back from asserting its new international status (which reflected the post-Cold War balance of power) too blatantly. I believe that if the first President Bush had won a second term in the November 1992 presidential elections, the world would have seen then what it saw when the Republicans regained power in January 2001; the group of right-wing conservatives at the helm of the Republican Party are more direct than anyone else in America when it comes to dealing with the realities of power.

During the Cold War, the contrast between the value system prevailing inside American society and certain aspects of its foreign policy was disconcerting to outside observers. On the domestic front America upheld values that had helped make it one of the most advanced societies in the world in all fields. It could rightfully claim an impressive level of democracy, a rate of economic productivity higher than one quarter of the entire global productivity, a vibrant culture, pre-eminence in the fields of science, technology and research and the strongest military force in the world. But America did not uphold the same values when it came to its dealings with the outside world. Justifying its actions as dictated by the conditions of the Cold War, American foreign policy had no qualms about maintaining friendly relations with corrupt and despotic military juntas in Central and South America, as well as with equally unsavoury regimes in Africa and Asia. It also supported and used radical forces with extremist views, including groups, organizations and countries it now regards as enemies.

One of the most important results of the Cold War culture is that US foreign policy lost sight of the fact that democracy is not only a human right for all the peoples of the world (including those of the Middle East) but that it is also the only safety valve that can protect humanity from the scourges of despotism, totalitarianism and extremism. During the Cold War the United States was occasionally concerned with upholding democracy and human rights, and with combating despotism and corruption outside its own borders – but only when it served its interests to do so. However, it turned a blind eye to blatant human rights' violations and abuses, as well as to glaring manifestations of corruption perpetrated by friendly regimes or those with which it had common interests. A deep crisis facing many countries today is that the United States has suddenly taken upon itself to introduce democracy, by force if necessary, into societies it was content for many years to leave at the mercy of corrupt and tyrannical rulers, whose subjects were brainwashed into believing that national pride entailed standing up to the challenge of Western civilization.

America's newly assertive stance as the unchallenged custodian of world order has not been met with universal favour. Not everyone is willing to accept that the new situation is an inevitable result of the seismic shift in the global balance of power. There are those who dispute the right of the United States to lay down the political and economic rules governing our world today, and others who question whether expressions like 'sovereignty' and 'international legitimacy' still have any meaning. While these questions and reservations deserve serious tackling, there is another set of questions that the Arabic world ought to endeavour to answer, far from its historic love of 'big words' that are mostly entirely isolated from reality:

- Is the policy of resistance, defiance and confrontation a means to an end or an end in itself? If the latter, what are its material repercussions? And if it is a means, what are its chances of achieving the end to which it aspires?
- Does a society's rejection of reform, development and modernization imposed on it by others reflect its understandable resistance to foreign interference, or does it reflect a rejection of those processes in absolute terms? Can any society avoid the imposition of reform, development and modernization by external forces without that same society initiating such processes itself in response to the aspirations and needs of its own people, rather than in compliance with the demands of foreign powers?
- In the early 1990s a major power in the region, Syria, raised the slogan of 'development without change'. Although developing without changing is a contradiction in terms, none of our intellectuals bothered to question what the slogan meant, or to look into the reasons behind our culture's opposition to change in any sphere, be it political, economic, management, social, cultural, educational or the mass media.

The previous chapters were meant to explain those reasons; starting with the blind allegiance of the Arabs to religion and to their rulers, which made the peoples lose the sense of their own identity, and of the depth and strength of their culture. It has made them live in fear of being invaded by the culture of the rising powers, a fact which raised a barricade isolating them from reality. They have locked themselves in a prison of intolerance, blinded in its darkness to their misconceptions and to what the 'Other' can bring. Barren of the dynamics of criticism and compromise, saturated with apathy, confined to void talk and praise of a glorious past which never was, they let their souls be invaded by the destructive evil of false belief that they are devoid of problems and that it is the 'enemy' that conspires to put an end to them. Hence, they are hostile even towards their own fellow citizens who have the misfortune of not belonging to the majority.

No wonder, then, that the Arabs' mentality remains confined and their soul barricaded in their own bound culture: the vicious circle keeps revolving.

What does that luminous disc
Do to my homeland?
The land of the prophets,
The land of the simple,
The chewers of tobacco, the dealers in drugs?
What does the moon do to us,
That we squander our valour
And live only to beg from Heaven?
What has the heaven
For the lazy and the weak?
When the moon comes to life they are changed to corpses,
And shake the tombs of the saints,
Hoping to be granted some rice, some children ...[2]

Nizar Qabbani

NOTES

1. An unexpected attack launched by the Japanese navy against Pearl Harbour, the US naval base in Hawaii in 1941, during the Second World War.
2. Author's translation from Arabic.

Epilogue

There might be many political, social or cultural phenomena which can hamper Arab culture (and hence most Arabic-speaking societies) and prevent it from catching up with human development or progress and from actively participating in these processes.

The two keywords in solving this problem are 'religion' and 'education', which must be understood here in the most negative, backward and hampering context of systems unable to either face or meet the challenges of this modern era and actively contribute to them by practising human creativity. These two factors are the main causes of the isolation of contemporary Arab culture from evolution and human modernization.

I would like to emphasize the closely knit relationship between these two destructive factors. While the culture of a backward and enchaining understanding of religion creates and produces a general climate which impairs educational levels and aids in its further deterioration, the educational systems originating from this era suspend human creativity which, in turn, results in more segments of the society adopting the diffident and medieval, dismal and austere interpretation of religion.

After finishing this book, the reader may wonder about the role of political tyranny, oppression, corruption and other manifestations of different oligarchies in this ghastly concoction, a cultural climate full of negative fixations and rich in deterioration and disintegration, hampering human minds from creativity, originality and ingenuity. My answer is that all these negative phenomena are not the problem but rather its symptoms. I do not dispute the existence of an obvious relationship between the cause and its symptoms. Tyrannical and despotic rulers definitely benefit from silencing the disapproving voices and shutting down the critical minds of their societies and communities. That does not however account for the proliferation of *taqlid* (blind following), senseless obedience and mindless imitation, which in turn is espoused by a backward interpretation of religion that aids this political tyranny.

The remaining – and vital – question is, 'Where do we start?' My answer can be summed up in one single phrase, namely: 'quality leadership'.

Humankind has seen two main courses of development. The European course, which can be described as 'simmering on a low flame' and which took many centuries to crystallize, and the Asian course, which can be described as 'fast cooking on a high flame'. In the first course, the maturity and evolution of democracy played a big role in hastening development, innovation and prosperity. The Asian model, on the other hand, started with quality leadership and then democracy found its roots in combination with growth and development.

It is important to elaborate on what I mean by democracy here. I do not mean ballot boxes or elections. Limiting and reducing democracy in backward and retarded societies to electoral processes and ballots results in destructive choices (for example, Hamas's victory in the Palestinian elections). I do mean democracy in its comprehensive overall definition, including the democratic culture, numerous parties, modern dialogue, democratic institutions, effective urban societies, constitutional and modern laws, an independent judiciary, low illiteracy rates and finally elections.

That way it will be understood that the tragedy of the isolation of modern Arab societies from human development and evolution rests on two major factors in Arab societies, namely religion (in its prevailing interpretation) and education (in its existing backwardness) which both negate and hamper any progress towards creativity, innovation and originality of the human mind.

Bibliography

ᶜA. ᶜA. *Turath al-ᶜabeed* [The Heritage of Slavery] (Cairo: Al Maktab Al °arabi Lel Maāref, 1998).

ᶜAbdel Razzak, Mahmoud Ismail, *Al haraqāt Al Sirriyah Fil Islām* [Secret Sects in Islam] (Cairo and Beirut: Sina Lel Nashr and Mu'assassat al Intishar al ᶜArabi, fifth edn, 1997).

Abu Hanifa, *Al-Fiqh al-Akbar* [The Great Jurisprudence] (Santa Barbara, CA: White Thread Press, 2007).

———, *Kitab Al Athār'* [Footprints] (Santa Barbara, CA: White Thread Press, Turath Publishing, 2007).

Abu Zeid, Nasr Hamed, *Mafhûm al-Nass: Dirâsa fî 'Ulûm al-Qur'ân* [The Concept of the Text: A Study of the Quranic Sciences] (Beirut and Cairo: fifth edn, 1998).

———, *Naqd al-Khitâb al-Dînî* [Critique of Islamic Discourse] (Cairo: fourth edn, 1998).

———, *Ishkâliyât al-Qirâ'a wa Aliyyât al-Ta'wîl* [The Problematic of Reading and the Method of Interpretation] (Beirut and Casablanca: fifth edn, 1999).

———, *Reformation of Islamic Thought: A Critical Historical Analysis* (Amsterdam: Amsterdam University Press, 2006).

Al Bukhari, *Hadith al Bukhari*, available at: http://www.holyebooks.org/islam/hadith_of_bukhari/index.html

Al Sabeᶜi, Nasser ibn Suleiman ibn Saᶜeed, *Al Khawārij Wal Haqiqa Al Gha'iba* [The Khawarij and the Missing Truth] (1999), available at: http://www.istiqama.net/books/Kwarig_book.htm

Al-Hakim, Tewfik, *Al-Ta'aduleya* [Equivalence], available at: http://www.scribd.com/doc/137219/-

Al-Mawardi, *Al-Ahkam al-Sultaniyyah'* [The Sultanic Commandments], available at: http://www.almeshkat.net/books/open.php?cat=11&book=1216

Al-Rafay, Mustapha Sadiq, *'Ala al-Safud* (Beirut: Dar al Kutub al 'Ilmiyah, 2001).

Al-Shafici, Mohamed ibn Idris, *Diwan al Imam al Shafici* [Imam el Shafici's Collection], available at http://www.kl28.com/books/showindex.php?bID=22

Al-Shafici, Mohamed ibn Idris, *Al'um* [Mother] (Beirut: Dar Al-Kotob Al-Ilmiyah, rev. edn, 2009).

Al-Tabari, Abu Jacfar Muhammad ibn Jarir, *Jāmic Al-bayān ʿan Ta'wīl Āy Al-Qur'ān* [Commentary on the Quran] (Cairo: 1902/03).

———, *Tarikh Al Rusul Wal Mulūk* [History of the Prophets and Kings] (Albany, NY: The State University of New York Press, 1985–2007).

Aquinas, Thomas, *Summa Theologica* (Westminster, MD: Christian Classics, 1981).

Chomsky, Noam, *Hegemony or Survival: America's Quest for Global Dominance* (New York: Metropolitan Books, 2003).

Dewey, John, *Problems of Men* (New York: Greenwood Press, 1946).

———, *Reconstruction in Philosophy* (New York: Henry Colt, 1920).

Fawzi, Mahmoud, *Camp David fi 'aql Wozara' Kharijiat Misr* [Camp David in the Minds of Egypt's Ministers of Foreign Affairs] (Cairo: Madbouli Bookshop, 1990).

Feuerbach, Ludwig, *The Essence of Christianity* (1841), available at: http://www.marxists.org/reference/archive/feuerbach/works/essence/index.htm

Fukuyama, Francis, *The End of History and the Last Man* (New York: Simon and Schuster, 1992).

Hanna, Milad, *Hewār al Thaqafāt wa Qubūl al-Ākhar* [The Dialogue Between Cultures and Accepting the Other] (Cairo: Al-iclamiya, 1998).

Hegel, Georg Wilhelm Friedrich, *Elements of the Philosophy of Right* (Cambridge: Cambridge University Press, 1991).

Heggy, Tarek, *Afqar Marxia Fi Al Mizan* [Marxist Ideas in the Balance] (Fes: Al Nasr, 1978).

———, *Al Sheyouceya Wal Adian* [Communism and Religion] (Cairo: Dar Nahdat Misr, 1980).

———, *Tajribati Mac Al Marxia* [My Experience with Marxism] (Cairo: Dar al Shorouk, 1983).

———, *Ta'amulāt Filʿaql Al Misry* [On the Egyptian Mind] (Cairo: The Egyptian General Book Organization, second edn, 2003).

———, *Critique of Marxism* (Cairo: Dar al Shorouk, 1992). Second edn re-titled *The Imperative Fall of Socialism* (Cairo: Merit, 2009).

Hobbes, Thomas, *Leviathan* (1651) (Oxford: Clarendon Press, 1909).

Hukkām Misr [Rulers of Egypt] (Cairo: Dar Al Hilal, 2005).

Huntington, Samuel, *The Clash of Civilizations and the Remaking of World Order* (New York: Simon and Schuster, 1996).

Hussein, Taha, *Fil Shiʿr al Jahili* [On *Jahili* Poetry] (1926), available at: http://www.scribd.com/doc/2288049/-

Ibn Abdul Wahhab, Mohamed, *Al-Kabaair* [The Great Sins], available at: http://www.almeshkat.net/books/open.php?cat=27& book 1080

———, *Usul al-Iman* [Foundations of Faith], available at: http://www.almeshkat.net/books/open.php?cat=27&book=830

———, *Khamsūn Su'āl Wa Jawāb Fil ʿaqidah* [Fifty Questions and Answers on the Doctrine], available at: http://www.almeshkat.net/books/open.php?cat=27&book=730

Ibn Anas, Imam Malik, *The Muwaṭṭa* [The Paver] available at: http://www.usc.edu/schools/college/crcc/engagement/resources/texts/muslim/hadith/muwatta/

Ibn Hanbal, Ahmad, *Musnad* [Reference], available at: http://www.ekabakti.com/dosearch.php?txtSearch2=&topic=ahmad&B1=Search

Ibn Khaldun, Abd Ar Rahman bin Muhammed, *The Muqaddimah* [The Introduction], available at: http://www.muslimphilosophy.com/ik/Muqaddimah/Table_of_Contents.htm

Ibn Qaiyim Al-Jawzeya, *Ad-Dā'ī Wa Dawā'* [The Illness and the Cure], available at: http://arabic.islamicweb.com/Books/taimiya asp? book=62

———, *Al-Fawaid* [A Collection of Wise Sayings], available at: http://talk.islamicnetwork.com/showthread.php?t=13846

———, *Miftah Dar As-Sa'adah* [The Key to the House of Happiness], available at: http://arabic.islamicweb.com/Books/taimiya.asp?book=82

Ibn Rushd (Averroes), *Bidayat al-Mujtahid Wa Nihayat al-Muqtasid. English. Selections* [The Distinguished Jurist's Primer] (Leyden: Brill, 1977).

———, *Faith and Reason in Islam* (Oxford: Oneworld, 2001).

———, *Fasl al-Maqal fi ma bayn al-Shari'a wa al-hikma min al-Ittisal* [Relationship of Religious Law with Philosophy] (Cairo: Dār al-Ma'ārif , 1972).

———, *Kashf 'an Manahij al-Adillah fi 'Aqa'id al-Milla* [Islamic Doctrine and Its Proofs], (Egypt: al-Maktabah al-Maḥmūdīyah al-Tijārīyah, 1935).

———, *Tahafut al tahafut* [The Incoherence of the Incoherence], (c. 1180), available at http://www.muslimphilosophy.com/ir/tt/).

Ibn Taymiyah, Taqi ad-Din Ahmad, *Al Tafsir Al Kamil* [The

Complete Exegesis] (Beirut: Dar Al-Elfikr).

———, *Ar-Raddu 'ala Al-Mantiqiyyin* [Answer to the Logicians] (Beirut: Deutsche Kultur International).

———, *As-Siyāsah Al-Shar'iyyah Fi Islāh Al Ra'ie Wal Ra'iyyah* [The Jural Policy to Reform the Ruler and the Ruled] (Beirut: Dar Al-Kotob Al-Ilmiyah).

———, *Majmuᶜ Al Fatāwa* [Collected Fatwas] (Beirut: Dar Al-Kotob Al-Ilmiyah).

James, William, *Essays in Pragmatism* (New York: Hafner, 1948).

Kalmagy, Mohamed Rawas, *Mawsuᶜat Fiqh Al Laith Ibn Saᶜad* [Encyclopedia of Al Laith ibn Saad's Islamic Jurisprudence] (Kuwait: Kuwait University, *Majlis al Nashr al ᶜIlmy*, 2002).

Kant, Immanuel, *Selections* (Glasgow: Jackson, Wylie, 1927).

Khadduri, Majid, *Al Shafi'i's Risāla* [Al Shafi'i's Message] (Cambridge: The Islamic Texts Society, 1987).

Martineau, Harriet, *The Positive Philosophy of Auguste Comte*, available at: http://socserv.mcmaster.ca/econ/ugcm/3ll3/comte/Philosophy 1.pdf

Marx, Karl and Friedrich Engels, *Manifest der Kommunistischen Partei* [The Communist Manifesto] (London: 1848), available at http://www.anu.edu.au/polsci/marx/classics/manifesto.html.

———, *A Contribution to the Critique of Political Economy* (1859), available at: http://www.marxists.org/archive/marx/works/1859/ critique-pol-economy/index.htm

Mawdudi, Abul A'la, *Towards Understanding Islam* (New York: Best Words, 1998).

Mill, John S. and Jeremy Bentham, *Utilitarianism and Other Essays* (Harmondsworth and New York: Penguin, 1987).

The Holy Quran.

Qutb, Sayed, *Basic Principles of the Islamic Worldview* (New Jersey, NJ: Islamic Publications International, 2006).

———, *Social Justice in Islam* (Cairo: Maktabat Misr, 1953).

———, *Ma'alim fi'l Tariq* [Milestones] (Beirut: The Holy Koran Publishing House, 1980).

Rushdie, Salman, *The Satanic Verses* (London and New York: Viking Press, 1988).

Sen, Amartya, *Identity and Violence: The Illusion of Destiny (Issues of Our Time)* (London: W.W. Norton, 2006).

Toynbee, Arnold, *A Study of History* (London: Oxford University Press, 1934–1961).

Wahba, Murad, *Mullāk Al Haqīqah Al Mutlaqa* [Beholders of the Absolute Truth] (1998), available at: http://www.4shared.com/get/60456761/c59d98dd/___.html;jsessionid=AE0C5FE61B8D003E15DC2B8A5781E570.dc156

Yasin, M. Naim, *Book of Emaan; Basis, Reality and Invalidation of Iman According to the Classical Works of Ibn Taymiyah* (London: Al Firdous, 2004).

Zarabozo, Jamaal al Din, *The Life, Teachings and Influence of Muhammad ibn Abdul-Wahhaab* (Riyadh: Ministry of Islamic Affairs, Endowments, Dawah and Guidance, 2005).

Index

Please note that page numbers relating to Notes will have the letter 'n' following the page number. The prefix 'al' is ignored in filing order.